Vastu

The Ultimate Guide to Vastu Shastra and Feng Shui Remedies for Harmonious Living

Contents

Introduction

It's common for many people to view buildings from a purely practical perspective that nullifies all attempts to improve comfort, aesthetic value, or energy. If you've never heard of the 'sick building syndrome,' it's time to become more familiar with its definition and impact. According to the WHO, the sick building syndrome is like an illness or medical condition common to those living in the same building and whose causes are not apparent or obvious. The building is often associated with that problem because the more its tenants are away from it, the better their health becomes. The effects and remedies for sick-building syndrome will be explained in later chapters.

Many people find it hard to believe that simple inconsistencies in room design, building placement, and interior design can cause drastic imbalances in the flow of our lives. However, many correlations and surveys have proven the positive influence of Vastu and Feng Shui designs. Houses and offices built according to the natural laws suggested by these sciences were of great value to our quality of life.

In essence, Vastu Shastra is an ancient Vedic and cosmic science deeply rooted in the theory of the five elements of nature surrounding us. It considers materials, geomagnetic energy, space, wind, and a host of other important natural aspects to analyze the flow of energy going into and leaving our bodies. Vastu Shastra is one of the few ancient architectural sciences that paid a lot of attention to humans' relationship with their buildings. It has established profound connections between a healthy life and a harmonious home or workplace.

Beginners may struggle to dive into a traditional book on a specialized field of science created thousands of years ago. This book is a simple guide that familiarizes you with important concepts and practical applications to use them in your life and line of work. While this book isn't a strictly academic overview of Vastu Shastra or Feng Shui architecture, it blends the different practical uses with contextual backgrounds to offer knowledge to both beginners and people who have dabbled in this science.

The History of Vastu Shastra goes back several centuries, and it's no easy task determining its exact origin due to its ancient nature. The Varahamihira's Brihat Samhita is believed to be the first Indian textual source to hint at a codified science employed to design entire cities and individual buildings. While Feng Shui is often confused with Vastu Shastra with architecture, these two concepts are hundreds, if not thousands, of years apart. It's believed that Feng Shui rooted its practices around the original principles of Vastu. You'll be able to distinguish between Feng Shui and Vastu by the end of this book, as many comparisons are drawn, elaborating further on the core differences and similarities found in both schools of thought.

This book focuses on the latest findings, analytics, and science-driven data related to Vastu and Feng Shui. Even though they have been around for some time, many new concepts are being discovered and recently translated scriptures. It's always best to have an up-to-date view of Vastu if you're planning to put the knowledge to practical use or study it from a closer point of view. The modern approaches to these sciences can differ greatly from how they were originally taught, seeing how the modern world both extends and detracts elements that may not have been in circulation during the sciences' founding.

The concept of living in harmony with nature is no stranger to modern architectural schools of thought and design, but few systems can get in touch with the cosmic frequencies and Vastu can. True harmonious living starts from within and then extends outward to our homes and other buildings we typically spend time in (school, office, library). So, whether you're trying to build yourself a more natural environment or battling the sick building syndrome, this book should guide you through the journey with both ease and expertise.

There is no shortage of books that can provide you with tips on how to enhance your décor or add finishing touches to create a natural home design, but this book is more about utilizing Vastu and Feng Shui to transform mundane buildings into organic and vibrant structures. From design to destructive Vastu remedies, you'll be learning about the true potential of concentrated energy. Finding a balance between a fast-paced modern life and serenely flowing natural energy is not an easy task. It requires an imaginative approach to solving these enduring concerns, which this book will shepherd you through.

Whether you're a DIYer or simply interested in exploring the realms of Vastu and Feng Shui, you'll find step-by-step tutorials complete with detailed explanations of the purpose of the final goal. Planning, designing, building, decorating, and many other processes are considered to allow for a comprehensive read, whose concepts can be applied in almost every building or environment. You'll be able to calibrate the different requirements for each environment with accuracy, thanks to the categorization and independence of each chapter. When it comes to practical uses, you don't need every chapter in this book to achieve your vision since it's designed to work on an on-demand basis.

You'll notice various intersection points between Vastu and Ayurveda, an ancient Hindu medical science. The similarities between them stem from the same foundational concept; the five elements of nature. As you develop more awareness of Vastu's true effects and implications, you'll be able to combine interior design, architecture, food, herbs, and aromas into a balanced ecosystem that ensures your body is at its most optimal state of health.

Chapter 1: A Brief History of Vastu Shastra

Vastu Shastra, the most famous Indian architectural paradigm, is known for having considerable benefits in terms of balance, harmony, and prosperity. Since most westerners aren't familiar with this ancient art, many believe it holds no real merits. However, this could not be further from the truth. Vastu Shastra has carved a place for itself as one of the most influential holistic sciences. Because learning more about this art is the only way to dispel the myths that surround it, this chapter focuses on the origin of Vastu Shastra and the misconceptions it's commonly associated with.

What Is Vastu Shastra?

Perhaps the easiest way to understand Vastu Shastra is to translate the term into English. Briefly, the word "Vastu" means "architecture," while "Shastra" means "science." Vastu Shastra is the "science of architecture." This science is employed as a guide for construction to guarantee harmony with the five elements of nature, also known as "Pancha Bhoota." These elements make up earth, fire, space, air, and water. At its core, Vastu Shastra is the science of directions and placements, and it stems from the belief that placing these elements in any setting can directly affect the flow of energy in the space. Since this art was first established seven thousand years ago, it's fair to say it has had time to develop and become easier to understand. As opposed to its early days, Vastu Shastra isn't as hard to comprehend now or considered knowledge that only engineers and architectures can leverage. On the contrary, even the average person can use the principle of Vastu Shastra to increase their wealth, spiritual and financial, and live harmoniously with nature. To understand how Vastu Shastra links directions to natural elements, here is a breakdown of where every element should exist for ultimate prosperity:

Earth: With the principles of Vastu Shastra, earth is considered the most important natural element. Because earth surrounds us, it doesn't have an optimum direction. Now, for those looking to buy agricultural lands, the ultimate placement should be southwest, as this direction governs longevity, which helps the land stay in good shape and produces bountiful harvests for longer.

Water: Water comes in many forms, including ponds, rivers, oceans, and even rain. Northeast is closely related to prosperity and wealth, so, according to The Vastu principles, water should be a northeast element. Vastu Shastra's experts believe this placement to be highly auspicious.

Fire: Southeast governs food, cooking, and fire. Since fire is a southeast element, experts recommend that homeowners place their kitchens in this orientation.

Air: Northwest is closely associated with enmity. As per Vastu Shastra's rules, placing windows and doors in the northwest direction is a surefire way to release negative energy and keep a place properly ventilated.

Space: Space is the element that maintains the balance of any setting. To ensure that the energy in a specific place remains balanced, be it a house or an office, plenty of open space should be left at its center.

Who Should You Invest Time in Learning the Principles of Vastu?

As we've mentioned, Vastu Shastra is all about living in harmony with nature, which is why it's an art that all people can benefit from regardless of their education or financial situation. But those who are tired of stumbling over hurdles and feel like their life is not going the way it should, can make great use of Vastu, as the lack of harmony they feel might result from not being in sync with nature. Furthermore, people who are on the market for a house may also benefit from Vastu Shastra since it can help them make sure the proper flow of energy in their new home. It's worth mentioning that the effect of Vastu Shastra can be felt either instantaneously or after a while. So, you must be patient to reap the results you want.

The History of Vastu Shastra

Vastu has been a significant aspect of Indian culture for thousands of years. Perhaps the earliest mention of such art was found in the treatise called "Mayamatam," which was written by the architect Maya— an influential figure in ancient India. The treatise was later discovered in 1934, becoming the first inkling of Vastu Shastra in antiquity. The excavations in Harappa, which aimed to unveil the Indus Valley Civilization, also found traces that hinted Vastu Shastra's principles in creating buildings and sewers. Interestingly enough, this elaborate architectural planning only was widely employed in other countries in the nineteenth century. Moreover, Vastu Shastra is mentioned in Indian poetry, particularly in the two Sanskrit epics "Mahabharata" and "Ramayana", which explore popular ancient Indian tales. Since this science was first used to build temples in ancient India, there are many mentions of it in sacred Hindu texts, such as Garuda Purana, Vishnu Purana, Matsya Purana, Agni Purana, and Skandha Purana.

The Story of Vastu Purusha

The story of Vastu Purusha explains the origin of science's principles. Generally, there are two versions of this story. Here is a rundown of each version:

Version 1

Shiva, the third god of the triumvirate and the lord of destruction, was engaged in an arduous fight with a demon. Due to the sheer strength of the demon, Shiva was growing tired and sweated. The drops of sweat that fell from his forehead birthed a creature called Vastu Purusha. Because he was born out of struggle, the creature was immensely hungry and had an appetite for destruction. His rampage struck fear into the other deities' hearts who thought he would devour the whole universe. The creature was too strong to contain on their own, though. So, they sought Lord Brahma, the god of creation, to find a solution to that conundrum. Brahma pushed Vastu Purusha, making him fall, after which he and the other 45 gods prevented Vastu Purusha from standing up by sitting on him. Knowing he was defeated, Vastu Purusha begged for mercy, claiming that none of it was his fault, that he was created this way. Because Brahma was a merciful god, he let him live and helped him satiate his hunger by allowing him to receive offerings from the people living in the houses built on him. In return, he promised to offer them prosperity and guard their health. Although, if they didn't satiate Vastu Purusha, they would face the consequences of his wrath.

Version 2

Lord Brahma was experimenting with his powers, attempting to bring new creatures to life. He created a gigantic man with an insatiable appetite. Brahma didn't give the man a name, and he let him satisfy his hunger as he saw fit. The man grew in power and body to the extent that he cast a shadow on Earth. As his powers grew more destructive, Lord Shiva and Lord Vishnu, the preservers of creation, asked Lord Brahma to stop the carnage the man was causing. As he realized his mistake, Brahma rushed to request the aid of Astha

Dikapalakas, the gods of the eight directions, to help him take down the man. Other gods also joined in the fight, and they all pinned the man facedown. The man cried and begged for mercy. Lord Brahma was not known to kill any of his creations, which was why he gave the man the name "Vastu Purusha" and asked him to guard the families' prosperity that built structures on him in exchange for taking gifts from them to ward off his insatiable hunger. Just like the first version of the story, Brahma allowed Vastu Purusha to punish those who failed to extend offerings.

As you can deduce, both stories focus on keeping Vastu Purusha satisfied by implementing the guidelines of Vastu Shastra. Harmony and prosperity are always the results of following these rules. But disregarding them means angering Vastu Purusha and facing adversity.

Myths About Vastu Shastra

Vastu Shastra and Feng Shui; Two Sides of the Same Coin

Since both concepts focus on the art of placement, some people confuse the Indian science of Vastu Shastra with Feng Shui. Feng Shui not only originated in China, but it's also a lot younger than Vastu Shastra. While Feng Shui draws on the principles of Vastu Shastra, it disregards some of Vastu's natural elements, such as space and earth. Vastu Shastra places more emphasis on concepts like weight distribution.

Vastu Shastra Is Superstition

Many propagate the belief that Vastu Shastra is merely a superstition built to trick people into thinking that their lives can change drastically by implementing its guidelines. This is just a misconception. Vastu Shastra is real science; it's built on astronomical and architectural knowledge. There's a spiritual dimension that goes into Vastu Shastra , but it isn't an integral part of it. It goes without saying that this science's principles aren't a magical remedy to all your problems, but following them can still have a positive impact on your life.

You Must Use Indian Furniture to Properly Implement the Rules of Vastu Shastra

Even though Vastu Shastra is an Indian art and practice, you mustn't limit yourself to Indian furniture when designing your space. Vastu Shastra is simply the science of placement, so it is where you put your furniture, not where it comes from, or what it looks like. If you are a fan of the rustic chic, bohemian, or even gothic aesthetic, choose the pieces that strike your fancy. Just be careful to follow Vastu's Shastra's rules of placement.

Feng Shui and Vastu Shastra Can Be Used in Tandem

Because Feng Shui and Vastu Shastra are both placement systems, there are people who think that using them together is the best course of action. However, this can do more harm than good. While the two systems might share several similarities, some of their rules contradict each other. So, it'd be wise to stick to just one system instead of blending two design paradigms fundamentally different.

The Principles of Building Vastu Temples

Most Indian temples are built according to the guidelines of Vastu Shastra, but before we give you examples of these sacred places, you need to know some of Vastu Shastra's rules for building temples. These go:

Shrines and entrances must face the East since it's the direction in which the sun rises. This gives it holy prominence.

Temples can have up to four entrances, with two in the east and the remaining ones facing north. But if the temple has only one entrance, the first rule applies.

The plot of land the temple will be built on should always be square-shaped or rectangular because circular, triangular, oval, or any other irregular shape is inauspicious. These shapes encourage the flow of negative energy and are considered unfavorable.

Water fountains should be placed in the east or northeast because these directions are closely related to wealth and prosperity.

If the temple has a kitchen, it must be in the southeast because this is the fire element's direction.

Temples Built According to Vastu Shastra's Principles

As you now know, most Indian temples follow the rules of Vastu Shastra, but perhaps the most famous one is Tirupati Balaji Temple. This engineering marvel was built in 300 AD as a testament to the outstanding legacy of Vastu Shastra. With over 40 million yearly visitors, Tirupati Balaji Temple remains one of the most praiseworthy creations of Vastu Shastra. Its foundations are still as strong as they were almost 1700 years ago!

In the Himalayas, Kedarnath Temple is another product of Vastu Shastra. Destructive floods left the towns near the temple in ruins. Surprisingly, though, Kedarnath Temple was not affected one bit. This proves that the principles of Vastu Shastra are the key to establishing long-lasting buildings that can stand tall in the face of natural disasters.

Vastu Shastra is a brilliant system and philosophy to investigate to achieve harmony in your life. Given its long history, it's a tried-and-true method of ushering in prosperity and wealth. Now that you know more about it, it's time to implement its guidelines to organize your house and workplace. Keep reading to learn more about these unique principles.

Chapter 2: Basic Feng Shui Principles

Feng Shui is an ancient Chinese philosophy that brings balance and harmony between elements. You may have preconceived ideas about Feng Shui, like how you can optimize the elements in your western décor. But that's only the half of it, as it can also bring positive energy, balance and promote energy flow to your physical and mental health. Because we're only familiar with furniture placement in terms of interior decoration, the thought of deriving energy from spatial arrangements can strike as a novelty. In the following chapter, we will explore this phenomenon and discover how you can implement Feng-Shui to leverage this energy in your home or workspace.

What Is the Chi?

Before we delve into the details of Feng Shui, there are basic concepts we need to understand first, such as Chi. In the practice of Feng Shui, Chi is the universal energy that permeates everything around us. It exists everywhere, both inside and outside man-made structures. Chi energy can have different forms, like Prana, Life Force, Ki, or Qi. Since it's a spiritual energy that can be channeled through different vessels, Chi can have multiple expressions that range between the positive and the negative. As for your body, Chi energy can move through three *dan tiens*, or three gateways: the heart region, the pelvic area, and the third eye center. You may have touched on this subject in your yoga class, as Chi is often employed in spiritual exercises.

The word Chi is of a Chinese origin, while Ki is Japanese, and Prana is Indian. Because this energy is purely spiritual, it is controlled via intangible channels and is harnessed through your body. Chi energy lies far from what we understand about the scientific energy and how it's harnessed. Chi energy cannot be converted into physical energy that can be used and measured in concrete, scientific terms. It can only be felt as you focus on your body, something which you can achieve through spiritual exercises, such as yoga or meditation.

Different Expressions of the Chi Energy

One of the most common expressions of the Chi energy is found in Yin and Yang characteristics. It can exist in two contrasting energies with the same origin. Another one of its manifestations can be sensed in the energy circulating throughout your body. This energy can be channeled to specific organs or limbs if you divert your mental faculties to that area. In doing so, this body part's temperature will rise, which proves the truthfulness of the Chinese saying, "Chi follows Yi," as Yi is your attention or focus. You can also find various expressions of the Chi energy in martial arts, yoga, orgone therapy, reflexology, pranayama, and chi kung. Because these practices were developed to enhance their users' mental and spiritual faculties, Chi energy will always be present in such activities.

What is Feng Shui?

Now that you know that the Chi is an integral part of the Feng Shui, you can better understand how to leverage it. Feng Shui mainly focuses on implementing harmony in one's environment. This harmony will channel out the Chi energy to the area surrounding this environment, which will affect people within the vicinity. Feng Shui can bring positive changes to the environment once the placements and adjustments are made correctly. It will influence space, landscape, and time. Harmony between elements brings balance, much like the balance between the Yin and the Yang. Feng Shui also aims to instill a sense of balance between man and nature and between Chi and the five elements. In Mandarin, Feng means 'wind,' while Shui means 'water.'

The Three Basic Concepts of Feng Shui

1. Yin and Yang

The concept of Yin and Yang is relatively straightforward. As you may already know, it implies continuous change, harmony, and a connection between two contrasting elements. It creates balance and acknowledges it as an essential and formative process of nature. The Yin-Yang symbol is central in Chinese philosophy and has been an important part of the Chinese culture for centuries. An example of the Yin and Yang energy is inner and outer energy, light and darkness, and movement and stillness. A combination of two contrasting elements will create harmony and stability, creating an equilibrium. This balance can be tampered with once one element overpowers the other.

2. Qi

While people interpret the Qi as another expression of the Chi energy, others believe it to be another spiritual force that is the product of abstract and real elements, like sunlight, color vibrations, air movement, water flow, our thoughts and feelings, etc. Invariably, this energy will affect how we feel in a certain place according to how harmony and balance are incorporated.

3. The Five Elements

In the eyes of a Feng Shui practitioner, the world comprises five elements, all of which must be in harmony to make a room feel proportionate, peaceful, and spiritually soothing. If these elements are not balanced well, the room won't harbor a positive and energizing appeal. It is important to take these five elements into consideration the next time you arrange your room or any habitable space:

Wood: It symbolizes creativity, strength, flexibility, intuition, and strength. Too much wood will evoke stubbornness and rigidity, while too little of the element can create stagnancy and depression.

Earth: This element generates feelings of balance and stability. An earth-balanced space can make you feel grounded, secure. If that element is overabundant, it will evoke heaviness or seriousness. Too little of that element will instill disorder and chaos.

Fire: Unlike the two previously listed elements, the fire element will spark enthusiasm and may even improve leadership skills. It is a symbol of boldness, inspiration, and creativity. Too much of that element can increase impulsiveness or aggressiveness, whereas too little can make you lack creativity and experience coldness and low self-esteem.

Water: Wisdom, emotions, and insightfulness come from this element alone, which is why it must be balanced in any environment in which it is placed. When water exists in great quantities in an area, it can make you feel socially overwhelmed. In contrast, too little of that element will evoke feelings of loneliness, isolation, and apathy.

Metal: Logic and clear thinking are typically associated with this element. If there's too much metal in a room, it will make you overly critical and reckless, while too little of this element will hinder your critical thinking abilities.

Through these five elements, you can achieve Yin-Yang balance and channel Qi energy properly through space. This is why you must balance out each element delicately. For example, the wood must be placed in vertical shapes so it can mimic the appearance of tree trunks. The wood shade should vary between browns, greens, and blues to resemble the colors of leaves, the sky, and flowers. You can also use house plants and miniature trees in your areas, such as the Lucky Bamboo or peonies, to achieve this. Wood furniture, fresh flowers, and natural fabrics will help you strike this equilibrium just as well.

The Earth element will make you feel grounded and promote a sense of stability. To achieve balance in this element, you must use decoration items in earthly tones, like blue, green, yellow, red, and brown. You may also use images of natural landscapes, such as beaches, forests, or mountains, and hang them on your walls. A room with a low profile kept to the ground will also help you achieve this balance.

Fire is very dynamic, so you must be careful with that element's placement to strike an ideal balance. Many homeowners simply exploit natural sunlight and use candles, but you can improve that balance with incandescent light bulbs and electronic equipment. Decorative pieces in red and golden shades can also be great assets to accomplish a fire harmony.

To incorporate the water element into any space, you'll want to add dark, deep, and glossy tones. You can use reflective surfaces as well by adding mirrors, but you may also integrate gazing balls or any other reflective surfaces for that purpose l. Wavy or asymmetrical shapes will help create water balance. If you're a fan of fish tanks, fountains, or water features, you can use them to create that balance.

Metal balance can be easily achieved through various elements. For example, you can use anything made of metals, like aluminum, iron, silver, copper, or bronze. You may also scatter around rocks or stones if you have decorative pieces made of these materials. Neutral and pastel colors can be effective, so integrate them into the room's color scheme.

The Bagua Map

Feng Shui practitioners use Bagua maps for décor plans. It's ideal for analyzing energy in any given space and giving you useful pointers on which elements require more emphasis to strike an elemental balance. The Bagua map comprises nine quadrants, which include elements and colors associated with these elements. These quadrants typically pertain to wisdom, career, love, fame, wealth, health, and people. If you don't know how to use a Bagua map, you can simply lay it over your floor plan such that it displays the nine quadrants and the alignments of the room. These maps are often used on floor plans, but you can just as well use them in smaller spaces.

Vastu Shastra vs. Feng Shui

Similarities

As established, Vastu means 'architecture' or 'dwelling,' and Shastra means 'science,' whereas Feng means 'air' and Shui means 'water.' Nevertheless, the differences between these two concepts extend way beyond semantics. Both have a common origin and are based on the belief and study of cosmic energies. Their philosophers believe that permeating energy (Chi and Prana, respectively) controls the flow of energy through spaces and even the human body. Both concepts posit that the center of any house is a powerful pool of energy where the force of all elements combine and intertwine. Vastu Shastra and Feng Shui suggest their own remedies to fix energy imbalances in any space.

Differences

As mentioned earlier, Feng Shui is rooted in the belief of existing spiritual energies, while Vastu presents a scientific basis to it. Feng Shui also focuses on geographical considerations for optimal effectiveness. It also works on creating a more conducive way of life by increasing the amount of positive energy in your home. In contrast, Vastu Shastra's theory dictates rules for building homes, as evidenced by the guidelines for constructing temples, which were laid out in the previous chapter. Color schemes for a house according to the presets Feng Shui are soothing pastel colors like cream, white, and beige, while color patterns of the Vastu Shastra guides range between bright colors, such as red and yellow. Moreover, the south is considered the most auspicious direction for Feng Shui, while the Vastu Shastra holds that the north is the best orientation and is a source of magnetic energy.

Chi and Prana

People believe these two energies are the same, much like God in Abrahamic religions. While this belief might have some truth to it, there are still subtle differences between them. Chi is a life force that finds its origins in early traditional Chinese medicine. It moves through the dan tiens, which work like the chakras, but they differ because they only pass through three gateways: the pelvic area, the heart region, and the third eye center. Prana works similarly to the Chi, but it comes from ancient India's Ayurvedic and yoga traditions. It also moves through pathways called the nadis and is commonly associated with the seven chakras.

You can now see that both the Vastu Shastra and Feng Shui present comparable qualities, as they both operate in similar ways and similar harness energies. However, it is up to you to explore both of their fascinating theories, parse through ancient philosophies, and follow either of these traditions. Once you delve deeper, you can decide which one resonates with you the most and integrate it into your home and lifestyle.

Chapter 3: Harmonious Living: The Modern Perspective

Our houses are our safe havens. The outside world is fast-paced, loud, stressful, and crowded. The only place we must relax, and recharge is our homes. Since we've strayed away from taking good care of our living spaces, the percentage of people affected by sick building syndrome (SBS) is on the rise. Paying attention to your home's design while factoring in balance, color, and harmony is primordial. This comes naturally to many people. However, what most homeowners fail to achieve is a proper spiritual balance in their homes. Harmony and unity are perhaps the most important aspects that anyone who is interested in the interior design must know. To re-invite harmony into our homes, it's important to step back and get back to basics. For this, we need to identify and understand the problem at its root.

What is Sick Building Syndrome?

This syndrome is largely prevalent in people who've just moved into a new place. Have you ever changed homes only to notice that you're constantly getting sick? You might catch the flu back to back or suffer from chronic exhaustion. Recurring symptoms of illness or general feelings of unease that keep getting worse with time are obvious signs you are experiencing SBS. Typically, the severity of the symptoms increases the more time you spend in the building. People may even notice an immediate relief once they step out of their new living environment, albeit temporarily. It's also worth mentioning that the syndrome isn't just limited to houses; SBS can manifest itself in corporate offices, apartments, and all sorts of buildings or structures. However, when the syndrome is linked to the place where you should be relaxing and resting, this can become highly detrimental to your physical, mental, and emotional health. In-office settings, SBS might cause a marked lack of productivity, an inability to focus, physical issues, and an overall disrupted work performance. This condition is commonplace in buildings where occupants begin noticing minor symptoms and signs until they get worse and face great setbacks in their professional and personal lives. It's been estimated that nearly 30% of new, renovated, or remodeled buildings, residential or commercial, can engender this issue for occupants.

Sick Building Syndrome Symptoms

It's no secret that we spend most of our days indoors nowadays, be it the office, university, school, home, or else. This means that our likelihood to develop SBS is now higher than ever. Sick building syndrome can be identified when a group of people (neighbors, coworkers) shares the same symptoms, with a frequency more than what is normal, and without an obvious explanation for their uneasiness. Usually, the symptoms' acuteness varies from person to person and according to the duration spent in the building. Among many, the most common symptoms include red, tired, or watery eyes; irritated, runny, or congested nose; difficulties in swallowing with irritation in the upper airway, a sore throat, and frequent rash and skin irritations. Other symptoms that can hinder your productivity and wellbeing are lethargy, migraines, irritability, along with diminishing concentration, and a shorter attention span. These symptoms do not impact a person's performance at work, the state of their relationship, and their sociability. They also take a significant toll on their overall quality of life, both inside and outside the home. The real problem happens when the building in question is a daycare center or a medical facility, where occupants are likely to be more vulnerable. This syndrome can also negatively affect the dynamics of workplace environments, translating into increased absenteeism, staff turnover, and crippled performance. While closing or demolishing offices due to SBS is rare, its consequences almost always lead to higher operating costs and loss of profit. The repercussions can be frightening. Reversing these symptoms is doable once you learn how to bring harmony and unity into any space.

Buildings and Climate Change

As much as we hate to admit it, our fast-paced, digital-dependent, consumer-based world is likely to toll the bells of civilization as we know it. Fortunately, a growing number of people are becoming conscious of their actions and the consequences they hold. Over the past couple of years, many have realized the true extent of our reckless, consumerist behaviors and their effects on the planet. More than ever, the only way to curb the global issue of climate change is by reducing our amounts of CO_2 emissions. While climate change and global warming are often used interchangeably, there's a key difference between the two terms. The former refers to the long-term increase in Earth's temperature caused by harmful man-induced activities, whereas the latter is a more general term that denotes the warming effect caused by both the planet's natural cycle and human activities. This endemic problem intensified in scope starting in the 1950s, at a time of post-war reconstruction and global industrial production. While the Earth's temperature used to increase only by 1-degree Celsius per decade, this has jumped to 1.2 degrees Celsius per decade ever since. Before 2020, it further increased to hit the 2.0-degree Celsius mark right by the outbreak of the COVID-19 pandemic. Through science and statistics, we've realize that humanity had to endure a sanitary catastrophe, which brought about paralysis and stagnation all over the world. This signals we collectively need to step back and get perspective on our planet's state. Restoring our bond with nature appears as the only viable way to curtail a potential global catastrophe.

Upon looking closely at the biggest pollution sources in our day-to-day lives, the damage is mostly taking place in our buildings and homes (aside from industrial production, global trade, transportation, etc.). A major part of addressing this problem is to analyze our own habits and patterns. This doesn't simply concern what we do in our houses and buildings, but it's also a matter of how our buildings are designed, constructed, the way we use them, along with the locations and types of terrain we choose.

Carbon Footprint

Two important variables must be factored in to reach an estimate of our buildings' carbon footprints. The first one pertains to the amount of energy that's generated and required for constructing and operating buildings. This accounts for roughly 36% of global energy use. The second aspect is the resulting emissions from daily activities, estimated at around 39% annually. Evidently, these figures should not be taken lightly.

Now, to understand the root of the problem, we need to consider two important parts that go into the equation. On the one hand, there's the day-to-day use of energy, which can also be called "operational carbon footprint." On the other hand, we find all the energy expenditure related to the manufacturing of building materials, the transportation of these materials to construction sites, the actual construction process, with all that it entails (electricity and gas use, machinery, labor, etc.). While the operational carbon footprint is virtually impossible to alter, the second aspect can be put under control by minding our actions and allocating resources properly. The carbon footprint of buildings that results purely from construction operations is expected to diminish by nearly 30% in the year 2030, all thanks to the Paris Climate Agreement that aims to limit the rise of global temperature rate only to 1.5 degrees Celsius.

What Can We Do?

Now that we have a better grasp of these contemporary challenges, we should take concrete action to put a stop to all the harmful practices we've engaged in for decades, intentionally or otherwise. A popular, deep-rooted belief states that reducing carbon and greenhouse emissions can only happen once we learn to exploit and control nature in newer ways. This couldn't be further from the truth. Such a conceited and human-centric approach ignores the fact that humanity is only a lost dust speck in the vastness of the universe and that the forces of the universe rule us, not the other way around. Nature simply cannot be tamed. Instead, we must bring harmony back into our lives and learn how to be in sync with our environment. Immersing ourselves in the beauty that nature holds will teach us how to deal more with our surroundings in smarter, more reasonable ways, rather than exploit them for luxury or profit. Ultimately, incremental changes and subtle lifestyle adjustments (energy saving, recycling, use of eco-friendly materials) can make a world of difference and help sustain the planet for decades to come.

Harmonious Living and Unity

While many people will confuse harmony" and "unity," but in truth, there is a major difference between these two concepts. On the one hand, you may think of unity as a design philosophy that seeks to establish patterns by using the same shapes, colors, and materials to put together coherent and balanced spaces. But harmony is the feeling of spirituality and 'sense' that you get from your house's design. This is when Vastu and other ancient paradigms prove their worth and relevance in the modern world. Nowadays, we need a touch of harmony and unity to turn our houses into homes that combine practicality, aesthetics, and relaxation while enabling us to connect with our surroundings.

Several people wonder why the look and feel of their homes are so bland and lifeless, despite having paid a fortune to perfect it and design it to their image. Seven essential principles help bring any interior design together; all must be in perfect balance with one another. Here is a brief run-through of each one:

Theme: Absent a unified theme throughout the house, you will feel chaos seeping in without understanding the real reason. A strong theme is the foundation of your design, in which every shape, material, and color work toward fulfilling.

Rhythm: Every house's rhythm manifests itself in repeated colors, patterns, as well as matching shapes and sizes. While maintaining the rhythm throughout the house is essential, some interruptions with focal points and colorful highlights can add depth and value to your design vision.

Repetition: When a certain element is recurrent throughout different areas of the house. Too little or too much repetition can affect your space in negative ways. The key is to focus on a singular feature of the house (a color, a piece of furniture, a décor item) which you like and place it in different rooms, but in moderation.

Continuation: In a similar vein, this element is achieved through the extension of a certain pattern or line in more than one area to bring these spaces together with a united sense. It can be the color of the walls, a wallpaper design, or the type of flooring. Integrating continuity is the best way to incorporate unity while retaining the uniqueness of any home.

Similarity: The major difference between similarity and repetition is that, with repetition, you are copying the same pattern, color, or shape again to reuse it in another area. In contrast, the similarity is the use of a specific design that seems repeated but shows a characteristic that makes it unique every time (notably geometric patterns). When perfecting this element, your house will radiate unity and balance.

Perspective: Finally, the element of perspective entails creating depth through different dispositions and arrangements, which makes a home's features stand out yet retain their unity.

Harmony and unity are two ancient concepts that still bear a lot of relevance, especially given everything the world is enduring. After understanding the fundamentals of these two concepts and how essential they are, we can delve deeper into Vastu's concepts and applications for harmonious and comfortable living.

Chapter 4: Vastu Shastra Essentials

In the previous chapters, we introduced you to the history of Vastu Shastra and how it remains relevant in today's world, along with the importance of harmonious living. In this chapter, we will walk you through the essential principles of Vastu Shastra and how each precept impacts the overall balance of energies in any space. As you'll come to learn, the different elements of Vastu complement each other to form a workable framework that you can apply to reap its benefits in all aspects of your life, from the home to the workplace. Without further ado, let's dig in!

The Importance of Energy Balance

Years ago, Albert Einstein concluded that everything we know and experience is pure energy. Everything around us, from objects to emotions and sounds, is all made up of energy. Even us humans, our physical and spiritual existence is an embodiment of an intricately balanced, energetic field. When this balance is disrupted, this is when we suffer, physically, mentally, and emotionally. This all brings us to the Vastu teachings and how their purpose is to utilize various features, such as colors and the directions of objects in any space, to restore the energetic balance of its occupants. With that in mind, we'll move forward to expand on the tools of Vastu Shastra and how they can effectively promote this harmonious balance of energies.

Despite being an ancient science, Vastu Shastra has developed into a comprehensive architectural concept used to design aesthetically pleasing and energy-inviting buildings to encourage healthy, conscious living. Modern-day Vastu Shastra can be better explained through five fundamental principles:

The 5 Main Principles of Vastu Shastra

1. Site Orientation-Diknirnaya: Directions and How They Are Perceived According to the Principles of Vastu

There is no such thing as a good or bad direction. In the Hindu culture, which is the main source of the Vastu principles, the activities we do in any space must be associated with a specific geographical direction to bolster its effects and bring prosperity. As you'll learn throughout this chapter, directions are the basis upon which all other Vastu principles are built. Unlike standard architects, a Vastu expert would reflect on these considerations before designing any property layout. It isn't just a matter of aesthetics or logical planning. To build a home or office that abounds with good vibes and leads to a happy life, it's imperative to learn the significance of each cardinal direction.

- **North:** This direction is all about career prosperity and material wealth. According to Vastu principles, this direction should be saved for bedrooms, study rooms, and water bodies.
- **South:** This one represents status and prominence. A manager's office or a master bedroom will be conducive to success if built facing the southern orientation.
- **East:** Known as the direction of the sun, the East suggests new beginnings and healing. It's the ideal direction for windows, doors, and gardens. Family rooms can also benefit from the warmth and health properties of this direction.

• **West:** Strength is the dominant quality of the western orientation. A home gym or a study should be built facing west.

Vastu is equally influenced by ordinal directions, detailed below:

• **Northeast:** For mental well-being and feelings of tranquility, pooja rooms and other spiritual activities should be directed toward the northeast. If you've been struggling with your yoga practice and haven't been able to be mindfully present, try changing your location to a northeast-facing space and notice the difference.

• **Northwest:** An airy direction best saved for toilets, bars, and it also works well for kitchens. Guest rooms should face this direction, since it's known as a zone of helpful friends.

• **Southeast:** Also called the zone of Venus, the southeast brings good health and is ideal for kitchens. This direction is equally suitable for spaces dedicated to artistic activities; children's art rooms or home studios can be more inviting and conducive to creativity when in the southeastern zone.

• **Southwest:** Heavy objects should face this direction since it promotes strength. Items like bulky cabinets and overstocked pantries should be facing southeast.

Understanding the meaning behind each direction is only the theoretical aspect of Vastu principles. In practice, you should be able to accurately find each direction in any room. A good way to decide the ideal purpose for a room is to use a compass with your back to its exit and noting the exact orientation. By using this simple technique, you'll be able to easily work out the rest of the directions, both cardinal and ordinal.

2. Site Planning-Vastu Purusha Mandala: How It Relates to Vastu Shastra

One cornerstone of Vastu Shastra is the Vastu Purusha Mandala. In Sanskrit, the word Mandala literally means "circle." The term can also refer to any diagram that can be a guiding tool in any endeavor, be it spiritual or architectural, as is the case here with Vastu Shastra.

Historically, Vastu Purusha Mandala first came about when Brahma promised its namesake monster a prayer every time a man builds a structure on Earth to compensate for his suffering after Brahma pinned him down and left him incapacitated. The Vastu Shastra Mandala diagram depicted this tale and was a reference point for the principles of Vastu Shastra. Legend has it there were 45 gods pinning down the monster Vastu Purusha, and their positioning influenced the significance of each of the cardinal and ordinal directions. Each god had their unique powers and represented unique qualities. For example, as you'll learn later in this chapter, the center of any structure should be kept wide open since the supreme Brahma was the one occupying the center of the Vastu Purusha Mandala. Angi, the lord of fire, was occupying the southeast direction, which associated it with passion and creativity.

3. Proportions of The Building-Maana

The right ratio between height and breadth must be respected for optimum functionality and a pleasant overall look to design effective and harmonious structures. The energetic balance element cannot be overlooked because, after all, Vastu is all about achieving this coveted objective. For many years, Vastu scholars worked hard to identify the perfect measurements to act as a guide for anyone who wishes to erect a well-proportioned building. Eventually, they named a set of ideal ratios of height to breadth that can be applied universally:

- A building with its height equal to its breadth is considered proportionate
- A building with its height 1.25 times the size of its breadth is said to be adequately stable
- A building with its height 1.5 times the size of its breadth is pleasant to look at
- A building with its height 1.75 times the size of its breadth is sturdy and beautiful
- A building with its height two times the size of its breadth is optimal

Abiding by the abovementioned construction ratios will guarantee balance, harmony, and consistency in neighborhoods and cities; they are ideal for creating proportionate and aesthetically pleasing structures and living communities in any urban setting.

4. Dimensions of The Building-Aayadi

A principle of Vastu Shastra identifies six essential formulas for deciding on the height, length, width, parameter, and area when designing a building to make sure it ends up beautiful. It goes as follows:

- The Yoni and Vyaya formulas can enhance the breadth
- The Aaya, Vyaya, and Raksha can enhance the length
- The Yoni formula can also fix the orientation of a building that wasn't initially designed with the cardinal directions in mind.

5. Aesthetics of The Building-Chanda

Chanda, which translates to 'beauty,' refers to a building's aesthetics. Vastu is a science that respects proportionality and logic. However, this comprehensive architectural system also minds the element of beauty and how a structure should appease both onlookers and dwellers. The Chanda principle makes it easier to identify different buildings far away according to their function and purpose. For instance, all temples were essentially shaped like mountains and are easy to locate. There are four main types of Vastu Chandas that can be used with building. These include:

- **Meru Chanda:** As seen on many Hindu temples, in Meru Chanda, buildings have a long, pointed top
- **Khanda Meru Chanda:** Here, the building doesn't have a uniform outwardly shape
- **Pataaka Chanda:** Buildings with a Pataaka Chanda resemble a bird's wings spread wide open
- **Sushi Chanda:** In Sushi Chanda, a building has a needle-like pointed tip

What is Pancha Bhoota?

According to Vastu, elements are of paramount importance; each believed to inhibit a specific direction. As explained earlier, in the Vedic tradition, there are five elements in nature: earth, water, fire, air, and space. Each element represents a facet of human life, which, if kept in balance, will promote Zen, healthy, and prosperous living. Below, we analyze the importance of categorizing the activities you do and the objects that surround you to understand how you can combine directions and elements for optimum results:

- **Earth:** Heavy objects that share the yellow and brown shades of soil and stones are considered earthy items. For instance, a chest of drawers made of wood or a stone sculpture is earthy objects, and they're best paired with the southwestern direction that will promote stability and grounding.

- **Water:** Humans have revered water since the dawn of time. This fundamental element symbolizes the essence of life and continuity. Vastu postulates that flowing water represents fluidity and avoiding stagnation. Remembering that, it's easy to see that with architecture and design, you'd want to locate any body of water (an indoor fountain or a swimming pool) in the northern wing of your home to heighten their effects.

- **Fire:** Fire is the element associated with power and influence. Matching your fireplace, stove, and other fiery elements with the south, this direction of prominence will intensify the positive effects in your home.

- **Air:** If you've ever wondered why an easy-going and pleasant person is described as "airy," it's because the air element is all about happiness and lightness. This element resides in the east, and when combined with its original inhabitant, the sun, it can bring about immense joy and an abundance of luck. When building your new home, doors and windows should always face east to keep the air element well-balanced.

• **Space:** Space is the element of central areas and signifies constant improvement. It's crucial to make way for energy to flow freely at the center of any place. The west direction is the recommended one for space elements. A foyer or a large hallway in an office should be kept clutter-free, and preferably with a high and sunlit ceiling for maximum positive energy.

While the information can seem overwhelming, with time, you'll be able to categorize objects around you into elements and find the perfect spot to place them. You can always use this book as a reference guide whenever you're confused about how to best combine different elements and directions in your home or office space.

The Importance of Colors in Accordance with Vastu Shastra

In Vastu Shastra, colors also play a dynamic role and are considered one of the essential principles of this science and art. You cannot possibly build a Vastu-compliant space without grasping the idea behind each color to be utilized in the best way possible. Different colors reflect different energies and are best paired with specific directions and rooms in any home. But since we all have our own preferences, there isn't a rigid, unified Vastu color code. Instead, we will discuss the main colors and generally show you how you can best use them:

• **Blue:** Blue is a color of relaxation and serenity. Since it's associated with water bodies, its properties can come to life in the northeastern direction. Painting a room a soothing shade of blue will help instill a feeling of calmness and relaxation. However, if blue walls do not match your room's theme, try adding blue accents instead. You can accessorize the room with blue décor items, cushions, or hang turquoise frames on the wall. Find the amount of blue that you're comfortable with, yet don't miss out on the amazing qualities of this iconic color.

• **Green:** The green color is perfect for promoting healing energy. Walls in hospitals and retirement homes are usually painted in therapeutic shades of green. According to Vastu, the north is the direction that works best with green. Using indoor plants can also capture the green color's healing powers if you've already chosen to go with neutral-colored walls.

• **Yellow:** Yellow is a happy color that is more impactful when used toward creativity, which is the southeast. Save this color for your kids' bedroom to spark joy and in your kitchen to emphasize the warmth in this cozy space.

• **Pink:** Pink denotes love, and when used in a southeast-facing room, can help improve intimacy and closeness between its occupants. Since pink is often stereotyped as "girly," you can choose pink accessories rather than paint an entire wall in pink.

• **Purple:** Purple is an omen of wealth and prosperity. It suits the south direction and can ease feelings of anxiety and depression.

• **Brown:** Last, brown and beige tones are the ultimate earthy colors. As one would expect, they come across particularly well in the southwest direction where the earth element resides. Under Vastu, using brown shades effectively brings stability and balance to any space.

Vastu Shastra is a wholesome architectural design philosophy that can be followed from the early inception phases of building. It's a thorough and all-encompassing system that anyone can apply and benefit from. The Vastu essentials that you've just learned in this chapter will come to life over the next chapters, where we will provide concrete actions and steps you can take to build or rearrange a home and workplace under the Vastu precepts.

Chapter 5: Vastu for the Home

Now that you understand more about Vastu Shastra and how it can help create an environment of prosperity and abundance in living spaces, it's time to learn how you can achieve it. This chapter will dig deeper into Vastu Shastra design precepts and give you plenty of ideas on how to incorporate them harmoniously and effectively. Whether your home is still in its conception or construction phase, or if you've inhabited it for a while, you can greatly benefit from the concepts of Vastu. And while Vastu Shastra can be applied in any space, this chapter's focus will be on the home since it's where people spend most of their time.

First: Applying Vastu Shastra During Construction

Starting with a clean slate will grant you a better chance to incorporate The Vastu principles into every corner of your house. Generally, all the rooms should be square or rectangular, with four cornered ceilings to attract abundance and joy. Here, we discuss how to use simple tips to make every room in your house Vastu-compliant. Let's get started!

- **Choose the Entrance Direction Wisely**

As per the Vastu science, the sun is considered the main source of positive energy. Directing your home entrance towards the east, where the sun rises will set you out on a great track to start. If you choose not to work with a specialized Vastu consultant, meet with your contractor before building the rest of the house. Given that your entrance is the main gateway for outside energy to penetrate your space, you need this to be a 'good door' to invite prosperity and keep away the negative vibes. Choosing teak wood for your entrance door can attract even more positivity. If you aren't building your own home and looking for a ready-to-move property, it's best to remember that and focus on finding a house with an east-facing entryway. Avoid property with an entrance facing southwest, since this is said to be the entrance of evil energy that carries struggles and hardships to the home dwellers. A southeast entrance is not any good either, as it's believed to be a direction that lets in sickness and anger.

- **Find the Perfect Location For Your Kitchen**

When choosing where to place your kitchen, Vastu teachings recommend a southeast direction for auspiciousness. In addition, the location of the kitchen in your house is just as important. You cannot have the kitchen facing a bathroom or a bedroom. For a propitious kitchen, walls should be painted in a bright color, like green or red, to create a pleasing aura. During construction, have at least a couple of windows in your kitchen since open windows let good energy in. Also, installing an exhaust fan will allow the room to ventilate and let the negative energy out. If you're leaning towards built-in electrical appliances, you must think about the placement of each. For the stove, which represents the fire element, it must be facing a southeast direction. But the sink is a water element that should be placed nowhere near its fire nemesis; a northeast direction works better for easy water-flowing. As for the refrigerator, place it facing a southwest direction, away from any corners.

• **Build Your Bedroom in the South Western Corners**

With the most important room in your house, namely the bedroom, be careful about its placement. Your bedroom is supposed to be your sanctuary, where you get to relax and rest after a long and exhausting day. A southwest corner is ideal for your bedroom to make sure you don't pave the way for the disrupting "agni" energy that governs the southeast, which promotes misunderstanding and violence between couples. Also, dedicate one of the southwestern facing walls to your cupboard, and make sure that they open towards the north to promote the flow of positive energy throughout the room. Ask your contractor to leave enough space for your bedroom door to open at a 90-degree angle; this makes way for prosperous opportunities for the occupants. Ideally, the walls should be painted in neutral and soothing shades of pink, blue, or gray.

• **Have a Spacious Hallway**

According to The Vastu principles, the center of the home is believed to be its beating heart. When planning your house's layout, include a spacious hallway in its center. As the place where all energies come together and their powers reach their peaks, you must create a pathway for the positive ones to come in and the bad ones to flow out. This will create a beautiful, pacifying harmony throughout.

• **Build the Perfect Pooja Room**

Since a pooja room is where you will be meditating and praying, you must think carefully about how you can optimize the good energies in there. Vastu Shastra precepts recommend avoiding basements or top floors for your pooja room; the ground floor is the optimum choice for this sacred spot. Also, the northeast orientation is the favored direction for your pooja room. If you have enough space, ask your contractor to account for a 2-door entryway and a threshold to keep ants and other bugs out of your sacred room. Similarly, plan to have a low pyramid-shaped ceiling for symmetry that will help you achieve a meditative state with ease. As far as selecting a color scheme for the pooja room, choose bright and serene colors that are peaceful to look at (pearl white, cream, pastels). Don't forget to install storage cabinets facing southeast to keep your pooja books and incense bundles neatly organized.

• **Select the Right Location For Your Bathrooms**

A bathroom shouldn't be built next to or facing your kitchen. Instead, it should be in the northwest or southeast corners of the house. Bathroom doors should be placed along northern or eastern walls. Don't only think about convenience and décor when deciding where to locate the bathroom fixtures. Toilets should ideally be placed a few inches above the ground; floating toilets are trendier anyway, so you shouldn't have a problem finding ones that will complement the aesthetics and spiritual value of your house. While on toilet bowl placements, it should be placed along the west or northwestern walls of the bathroom as it symbolizes waste-discarding. Just like your bedroom, Vastu principles encourage using light pastel colors in your bathrooms, such as light blues, grays, or plain white.

• **Pay Attention To Your Kids' Room**

Your kids' room should teem with warmth and love to encourage their development and growth. When you are first designing its layout, it's important to remember some important facts. The door to the bedroom should be clockwise to keep away the negative energy responsible for sibling fights and rivalry. Their beds should be facing no windows, doors, or mirrors. Just like in your room, best to keep mirrors away from the beds to avoid the reflection of bad energies. If you are placing bookshelves inside the bedroom, they should face northeast and be made from warm, auspicious material like wood. It's also a smart idea to have your contractor design custom built-in cabinets and extra storage solutions for your kids to keep their room clutter-free and avoid disrupting energy flow. However, don't be tempted to add a storage unit under their beds. According to Vastu principles, this can induce nightmares and disrupt prosperity. If your kids are old enough, consider involving them in building a Vastu-compliant home. This will encourage them and teach them the importance of keeping their rooms always tidy and clean.

Second: Vastu Shastra For Your Current Home

To reap the benefits of Vastu in your existing home, there are essentials you can incorporate for impeccable results. These are:

• Add Bamboo For a Healthy Life

In Hinduism, plants are a symbol of health and good fortune, especially Bamboo, a sign of vitality and well-being for centuries. Invariably, bamboo plants are a must-have for any home that follows the basics of Vastu. But there are guidelines for putting this lucky plant on display. Foremost, as an indoor plant, green bamboo poles best thrive away from direct sunlight, so place your bamboo plant in a see-through glass container in the eastern corner of the room. For ultimate prosperity, try to combine the five elements (water, metal, fire, earth, and wood). Adding a red-colored fiery ribbon on the wooden bamboo poles makes two of the elements, to which you can then add stones and coins in the water-filled vase to tie all the elements together. Make sure the bamboo poles are always well-watered and kept fresh; wilting bamboos can bring bad luck and misfortune upon a home's occupants.

• Having a Buddha Statue on Display

Regardless of your religious beliefs, if you have any in the first place, Buddha is a respected figure believed to signify prosperity and good luck. According to Vastu's science, placing Buddha figurines made of bronze has the power to attract positive energy into your house and ward off negativity and harmful energies. Even if your décor isn't necessarily oriental, Buddha figurines are always a nice addition, and they won't seem out of place when you feel their strong effects.

• Turtle Figurines

In the Hindu tradition, turtles are a symbol of longevity, which mirrors these reptiles' impressive lifespan. According to the Vastu precepts, decorating your family room with metal or mud turtle figurines will bring good luck and happy and lengthy life.

• Pay Homage to Ganesha

Ganesha, the god of luck in Hinduism, is considered a sacred figure for anyone who believes in the powers of Vastu Shastra. You can pay homage to Ganesha as you prefer. However, it's recommended to place the Ganesha statue in your home's entryway and on top of an elevated structure, such as a floating shelf or a marble column. If you have an extra room you dedicate as a spiritual space (like a pooja room), this would be an ideal place for your Ganesha idol. Place it a few inches away from the wall to allow for the energy to flow around it and shower you with its blessings.

• Bowl of Floating Flowers

In most Indian cultures, flowers floating in a bowl of water is considered an unmissable feature in any home. When placed near the home entrance, it sends fortunate wishes towards visiting guests and welcomes them with a pleasant and refreshing smell. Always remember to wash the bowl regularly, change the water, and replace the flowers when they've withered. In doing so, you'll be inviting good vibes into your abode and checking an additional box for a Vastu-compliant home.

• A Fish Tank

According to Vastu teachings, aquariums have the power to reverse the negative effects caused by Vastu defects. Such defects occur when people disregard the importance of an objects placement or the energy flow of their home. A fish tank placed in a southeastern direction should reverse these undesirable effects and promote harmony.

Ultimately, those are important tenets of Vastu Shastra you must remember when building, furnishing, and decorating your home. In parallel, you can incorporate several essential daily habits to make it fully Vastu-compliant. Here's a quick and practical run-through to achieve a harmonious and balanced life at home:

- Keep your entrance clear to avoid disrupting the flow of good energy. If you don't want to regularly pick up your kids' shoes, install a shoe closet to optimize the space, and make your life easier.
- Display Vastu-friendly art. Images of flowing rivers, fish, and waterfalls are all Vastu paintings that attract wealth and auspiciousness into your life. If living abroad is a dream of yours, you can express this by hanging paintings of flying birds or photographs of trains and cars around your house.
- With financial prosperity, Vastu principles suggest hanging wind chimes at the entrance of your home. Alternatively, you can place them at the entrance of your bathroom to trap in wealth and prevent its escape. But you should never place wind chimes anywhere around your bedroom, as this can summon unfavorable negative effects, such as illness and misfortune.
- Maintaining clocks around your home in good condition is believed to attract wealth and pave the way for lucrative ventures.
- Feeding birds is not only a kind act, but it's also one practice you can implement for Vastu Shastra. Placing a simple bird feeder on your porch or balcony will make the birds come flocking your way, bringing along all the good luck and prosperity.

• Where you place mirrors around your house can make a world of difference in the energy you attract. According to The Vastu principles, having a mirror over your bed will reflect negative energy and hinder prosperity. A mirror above your chest of drawers where you keep your valuable items can help grow your wealth.

• Using purple orchids, pots, and linens to decorate your home is one of the simplest ways for maintaining the flow of good energy throughout your home. Purple is the color of health and wisdom, which means the more you incorporate it into your life, the more it will pay you back in health and auspiciousness.

• Ventilating your bedroom by letting in fresh air and sunshine will cleanse your home's aura and prepare you to receive wealth and good luck. As such, it makes it a habit to open the windows every day to allow the air to flow through, bringing in the positive energy and evacuating the negative one. Even during cold winter months, you keep up this practice, even for a few minutes during the morning and evening. You're bound to feel an instant mood lift by breathing in the fresh air, both before and after a good night's rest.

• If you've been struggling with bad luck for a while and you're ready to turn that around, light one lamp beside your bowl of floating flowers or aquarium each night.

• Last, make sure the toilet cover is always always down and the bathroom door closed.

As you can see, there are countless ways through which you can instill a more Vastu-friendly home living. Even if the concepts seem foreign to western architecture and interior design, try for yourself to see how different your life will be when you carry out these Vastu principles. Don't be overwhelmed by the information and recommendations listed above. The beauty of Vastu is that you can start small, and once you understand the reasoning behind each of its basic concepts, you'll be ready for bigger changes. In the next chapter, we'll move on to the workplace and provide valuable insight on how to use the science and art of Vastu to turn your office into a space conducive to productivity, wealth, and prosperity.

Chapter 6: Vastu for the Workplace

As a business owner, you may be wondering about how Vastu Shastra relates to business. The guidelines the system offers are not just limited to residential areas, but they can also be used in offices, factories, hotels, or any other business venue. Applying the precepts of Vastu Shastra to the organization of your workplace can help you generate more profits, ensure harmony, and stem the negative flow of energy in it. In this chapter, you'll find easy-to-follow tips on how you can use Vastu Shastra to propel your business forward.

The Benefits of Vastu Shastra for Business

While Vastu Shastra on its own isn't a magical solution to all your business woes, following its principles can alleviate stress you and your team might be under. Since implementing the teachings of Vastu Shastra may entail changing the whole organization of your workplace, it only makes sense you might be interested in knowing more about the benefits you will reap by doing so. If you're interested in employing the rules of this art in your work area, check out these reasons why this is considered a worthwhile investment.

Achieving Clarity

In business, you always must be quick on your feet and adapt to changing market demands if you want your venture to thrive. Naturally, this is easier said than done. Making split-second decisions while ensuring that they serve your company's interests is more challenging than it sounds. Therefore, most business owners strive to achieve clarity, as this allows them to weigh their options quickly and come up with the best solution without dwelling on matters too much or crumbling under pressure. Vastu Shastra is a sure-fire way of achieving clarity because it eradicates the flow of negative energy and provides you with the focus and support you need for your business goals.

Generating More Income

Truth be told, money is always at the forefront of everyone's mind, and you'd be lying if you claimed otherwise. Finding ways to generate more profits is also something that many business owners put in a lot of time and effort into. What if we told you that you could double or even triple your income just by implementing Vastu Shastra in your workplace? Far from being unfounded superstitions, the precepts of Vastu Shastra will put your company on the right track, increasing its opportunities for scaling up and attracting more clients. Whether you have a shop or own a factory, you're bound to notice a considerable increase in your sales when you apply the teachings of this science to your work environment.

Inspiring Your Team

Work is hard and keeping your team of collaborators motivated can turn into a herculean task if you don't know what you're doing. Although there are countless tips online and productivity books that cover several methods of enhancing creativity and motivation in professional settings, they are never effective if not coupled with the teachings of Vastu Shastra. If you apply these tips without keeping the principles of Vastu Shastra in mind, you'll be basically disregarding the root of the problem, namely negative energy. The best way to boost workplace productivity is to look for the problem area and remedy it right away, and this can be done only by implementing Vastu Shastra. This art enables people to be more in sync with their souls and allows them to draw on the surrounding inspiration to come up with more creative and valuable ideas.

Eliminating Discord

Workplace quarrels are common, regardless of the scale of your company or the size of your team. Such fights are almost always accompanied by dips in production and sales, plus they create a negative work environment where people are not comfortable voicing their opinions. Even if your staff members are always in sync with each other, they might still feel stressed out, especially if their jobs involve sitting in front of a computer all day. Because these jobs usually make people restless and more prone to irritability, you must continuously find ways to bring your team together. To enhance the harmony in your company, consider applying the principles of Vastu Shastra. From the choice of color palette and lighting to furniture placement, Vastu Shastra covers all the essentials you need to give your staff a positive, inspiring, and supportive work environment.

General Vastu Shastra Rules for Business

Considering the abundance of benefits, Vastu Shastra entails, you might be now interested in learning how you can apply its teachings to your business. Before we delve deep into these principles, you can implement in the workplace, you need to know some of the dos and don'ts of business as per Vastu Shastra's basic tenets. These can be summarized as follows:

Do's

• Always make sure that you have a wall behind your desk because it fosters support. You can reinforce this further by adding pictures of mountains, which symbolize stability and strength.

• Declutter the area in front of your desk to create a sense of openness and trust.

- Pick only wooden furniture
- Get high-back chairs. They are not only great for your back, but they also denote support.
- Place plants and lamps in the southeastern part of your workspace to increase your wealth and career growth
- Keep your workplace well-lit to dispel negative energy.
- Fix or replace broken furniture and faucets right away because keeping them in such a state will induce negative energy.

Don'ts

- Don't hang pictures of water or fluids on the wall behind your desk, as this will undermine your support. Likewise, avoid any pictures illustrating crying people, violence, struggle, etc.
- Don't cross your legs because this repels growth opportunities.
- Don't buy furniture that comes in irregular shapes: circular, triangular, oval, etc. Instead, stick to sturdy square-shaped or rectangular pieces.
- Vastu Shastra for Offices
- If you have limited office space, it may be wise to use Vastu Shastra to optimize the place and bring in more clients. Following are some rules you can follow to make sure that your office does not exude negative energy.

Office Location

We've already mentioned how irregularly shaped plots of land attract negative energy. Now, if you still do not have an office, make sure that the area you're considering is rectangular or square. The office should also be in a populous area to increase prosperity and your staff's productivity, so steer away from establishing your workplace off the beaten track. Offices should face east because positive energy flows in this direction, which will make your business more prosperous. If you plan on adding a drinking fountain or any other water source, it should be kept in the northeast, as this is the direction of the element of water. Generally, avoid having stairs or any other obstructions in the middle of the office. As explained in an earlier chapter, this area should be left empty to allow the energy to circulate effortlessly.

To add mirrors, make sure that they are placed in the northern section of the office to help you generate more income. They play a big role in Vastu Shastra; offices should be painted in bright colors to promote liveliness and enthusiasm.

Where You Should Sit

You are the head of operations, and ensure that your desk is ideally placed. Business owners and managers should always face north when dealing with clients since the north is the direction of the deity Kuber, the lord of wealth. North also denotes career advancement. Therefore, as a business owner, you should make sure that your desk faces this orientation. Don't sit under beams because they support the whole structure; sitting under them can negatively affect your fortune, making it harder to bring in and finalize new deals. Also, avoid seating arrangements that cause your back to face doors because this can create an ambiance of mistrust. To foster support, make sure that you always have a wall behind you. If you work from home, make sure that your workspace is not next to the master bedroom. Finally, be extra careful about toilet placement by keeping them in the north or northwestern area of the office, just like you would at home.

Where Your Staff and Clients Should Sit

Keep your staff on the eastern side of the office, as the east is the direction of prosperity. The northeast is the direction of wealth and growth. You should make sure that your company's reception desk faces the northeast. Avoid putting any fire element in this direction, as it can cause accidents and attract bad luck. If you have waiting rooms, they should be in the northeast or northwest, which are the natural directions of water and air. This will reinforce the clients' patience by supplying them with a large dose of positive energy.

Vastu Shastra for Factories

If you own a factory or are building one, the following are the most important Vastu Shastra rules to remember.

Factory Placement

When building or buying a factory, make sure it is in the north or east to help increase production and make more profits. Plots of land broader in the front and narrower in the back, known as Shermukhi plots, also bring good luck. Keep the factory entrance in the east, remembering that it must be large enough to establish the flow of positive energy.

Machinery Placement

Your equipment is your real capital. And while accidents happen all the time in factories, you can mitigate this risk thanks to Vastu Shastra. In this spirit, you must place all-electric machinery in the southern or southwestern section of the factory, as these two directions are associated with good health. Keeping equipment in the south and southwest can effectively prevent accidents and common workplace injuries.

Product Placement

You might think that the location of your raw materials, finished merchandise, and inventory does not affect profits or how fast these products sell, but this could not be further from the truth. This is why stacks of raw materials should be kept in the southwest and septic tanks in the north or northwest. When stacking finished products, make sure these piles are placed in the northwestern area. This can help you release the negative energy that might be clinging to them and sell them faster.

Vastu Shastra for Hospitals

If you own or operate a hospital, saving as many lives as possible must be your only priority. Hospitals can harbor an abundance of negative energy, which is why you need to learn how to eliminate negative energy for the safety and wellbeing of your patients. If you're thinking about using Vastu Shastra in your hospital, here are some things you can do:

The Location of the Operation Room

A lot can go wrong during delicate medical procedures, and you must make sure that your operation room is void of any negative energy. With the placement of operation rooms, they should always be in the west. The west is governed by the deity Lord Varun, the god of stability, fate, and rain. By staying under his protection, your patients will have a greater chance of making a stellar recovery. Also, make sure that the operation room entrance is big to attract plenty of positive energy.

Ventilation

Adequate ventilation is not only good for patients' health, but it can also expel negative energy. You should always keep your patient's room well ventilated. This can be done by adding large-width doors or windows. However, be careful about placing these windows, lest you invite in more negative energy! As a rule of thumb, windows should be placed in the east, the direction most associated with the sun element.

Equipment Placement

Extensive medical knowledge is not the only thing that factors in patients' health and recovery. Ensuring that the hospital's equipment is in tip-top shape can also go a long way towards achieving this end, which is why the institution's storage solutions should reflect this. Just like factory machinery, medical equipment must be kept at ground level in the west or southwest to prevent accidents or malfunctions.

Recovery Room Placement

Guaranteeing speedy recovery is something that doctors typically care a great deal about. With Vastu Shastra, you can help your patients get back on their feet and enjoy precious moments with their families much faster. When setting up recovery rooms, make sure that they are in the southwestern portion of the hospital; this direction is strongly linked to good health and is governed by the demon Niriti and planet Rahu.

The Placement of Your Office

We've already covered how Vastu Shastra can be used to provide improved health for your patients, but what about your health? Rest assured, as the teachings of Vastu Shastra can also be beneficial for doctors, nurses, and hospital owners. If you can choose your office's location, always pick north or east because these directions can increase the flow of power and success. As always, avoid any irregularly shaped furniture and make sure that the room itself is rectangular or square-shaped. By doing so, you will attract many opportunities to prove your competence and further your career.

Vastu Shastra for Shops

Due to the spread of COVID-19, running a brick-and-mortar shop has become increasingly challenging. With social distancing rules and limitations to remember, you may not have enough time or resources to dedicate to implementing the principles of Vastu Shastra in your commercial business. But not only can Vastu Shastra help your shop stand out and catch the eye of more people, but it will also enhance its prosperity and longevity. However, check out the next few tips to learn how you can make your shop Vastu-compliant.

The General Organization of the Place

When you're renovating your shop, you may disregard the rules of Vastu Shastra for improving the overall aesthetic of the place. Although, this is a fatal mistake that can ruin your business, it's potential for growth and impact your profits. To add extensions to the shop, make sure not to alter the rectangular or square shape of the place because, as you're well aware by now, irregular shapes function as magnets of bad luck and negative vibes. And stack your product in neat piles and place them in the northwestern section of the shop. Also keep the entrance in the east or northeast to make the place more inviting. Regularly check to make sure that the doors do not squeak, as this can increase the flow of inauspicious energy. Your cash counter should be carefully installed so it allows it to open towards the north, the direction of the deity Kuber, the god of wealth. Finally, if you dabble in electronics, e.g., computers, televisions, phones, etc., keep these products in the southeast instead of the northwest.

Ultimately, the teachings of Vastu Shastra can be applied to all walks of life, including business. No matter your occupation or position in your company's hierarchy, the tips in this chapter will be of great help in furthering your career and leading a fuller, more prosperous life. Whether you want to seek help from a Vastu consultant or reorganize your work area yourself, make sure not to disregard the principles of Vastu Shastra because this might bring about adverse effects in the long run.

Chapter 7: Design Principles: Architecture and Interior Designing

Vastu Shastra might seem like an outdated concept. It's been around for thousands of years, and what might have worked eons ago doesn't apply to modern architecture. This also explains why many people are reluctant to implement Vastu design precepts in their work or living spaces. Regardless of what uninformed individuals may believe, Vastu Shastra still bears incredible significance today. In this chapter, you'll discover the benefits of this art in modern architecture, along with quick tips on how to apply its principles for more harmony and prosperity.

Why Is Vastu Shastra Still Relevant Today?

Even if you strongly believe in the ancient science of Vastu Shastra, it still might be hard to justify implementing its teachings in the 21st century. It also doesn't help that balancing its teachings and modern interior design trends can be challenging and costly. There are two different opinions. Architects believe that Vastu Shastra is just an old paradigm that holds little merit nowadays. But others think that Vastu can still be integrated into modern architecture despite being an old science. The second group seems to have it right, though. Since Vastu Shastra is based on Earth's magnetic field principles, cardinal directions, natural elements, and Prana (the Earth's energy), it qualifies as a powerful tool for achieving harmonious living. These elements are timeless, so they still affect us to varying degrees. Because such powers virtually haven't changed one bit throughout the years, you still need to heed the teachings of Vastu Shastra to stay protected and ward off negative energy. Therefore, we're inclined to say this art has not withered by time but has only grown even more vital.

Why Should Vastu Shastra Be Integrated into Modern Architecture?

Saying that art is still today usually isn't enough to incentivize people to try it. When money is a factor, most property owners should learn more about the concrete benefits before investing a dime in something. Now, if you're still on the fence about Vastu Shastra, here are reasons integrating its principles into modern architecture is well worth it.

Vastu Shastra Encourages Optimal Use of Space

Let's forget about Vastu's spiritual aspect for a while and think about how it can save you a pretty penny! While true that changing an already-established space to make it Vastu-compliant can be an arduous task sometimes, you'd be surprised at how much money it can save you. If you're thinking about up sizing to a bigger office or house, it might be wise to analyze how you're using the space you already have. Usually people who don't follow Vastu Shastra's principles end up with cluttered spaces that barely have enough room for their furniture and belongings. With Vastu, you'll be able to make the best use of any space, not just by decluttering it but by organizing it so it allows for more expansion, which is always a plus, especially for business owners. By integrating this philosophy into interior design, you may realize that there's to move to a bigger house after all! That quite a bit of saving, to say the least.

Vastu Shastra Is Easy to Implement

Given the many rules, Vastu Shastra has, implementing them may feel like you've bitten more than you can chew. With countless factors and placement strategies to remember, applying Vastu Shastra to your living or work area might seem downright impractical. But don't knock it until you try it! Vastu Shastra sounds like a complicated concept, especially to those who've never heard about it before. However, once you understand its core rules, implementing it becomes child's play. It all boils down to following its guidelines. Fortunately, Vastu Shastra's design principles haven't changed for millennia, which means you'll easily find plenty of professionals willing to help if you still believe you cannot handle it on your own.

Vastu Shastra Brings Financial Gains and Emotional Stability

Life is admittedly hard at the moment. With a pandemic on the rise, saving a few pennies here and there can make all the difference. What if we told you there was an easy way to markedly improve your financial situation? While applying the principles of Vastu Shastra isn't a guaranteed way of becoming wealthy, it does open many doors. Financial gain is one of the greatest benefits associated with this science. By encouraging the flow of positive energy, you'll reap many merits this comes with, including monetary ones. You're also bound to find yourself more at ease in a Vastu-compliant space. Since Vastu's main goals are to curtail the flow of negative energy, you'll let go of grudges and feel more satisfied with your life.

Vastu Shastra Builds Trust and Harmony

Whether you have a big family or run a business, you know how tension can get to people and make them fight over the silliest of things. Although many people think that quarrels among siblings and work colleagues are normal, have you thought about why they happen in the first place? Naturally, many of these misunderstandings can be attributed to ego or stress, but you cannot discount the energy that permeates the places where such arguments start. Places filled with negative vibes make people more irritable, quicker to jump to conclusions, and blame others. This is simply the result of ignoring the teachings of Vastu. The only way to remedy this is to investigate integrating Vastu Shastra into modern architecture.

Vastu Shastra Tips for Modern Architecture

Choosing Sites

To start implementing the principles of Vastu Shastra, start with the ones that relate to how you can choose auspicious sites. These are:

Soil

From a scientific perspective, the quality of the soil determines how strong a building's foundations are. Whether you're an architect or a would-be property owner, you must keep this rule in mind to choose a suitable, future-proof plot of land. When on the market for land, pick a plot with cultivable soil, even if you don't plan to grow crops once you buy it. The color of the soil itself can help you decide whether it is cultivable or not. Yellow, brown, and brick red soil are generally considered good for planting crops, whereas black and clay-like soil aren't. Now, how does the color of the soil or its potential for cultivability affect a building's foundations? Clay-like and black soil holds excess moisture, which can weaken the foundations of your property. Uncultivable soil also doesn't allow for good drainage, causing foundations to debilitate as time passes. Rocky soil, too, is a bad choice because you must pay extra to make it suitable for laying your foundations. Sites that are teeming with worms or have graves are off-limits as per the teachings of Vastu Shastra. Not only do these sites increase the flow of negative energy, but they also signal that the soil itself is loose, meaning it will not offer enough stability and support for your foundations.

Is there another way to assess the quality of the soil without depending on its color? Yes, there are two simple tests you can try to see if the soil is good enough as a base for your building. First, you can try digging a small hole, 2 x 2 x 2 inches, and fill it with water.

After an hour, check whether the soil has absorbed the water. If excess water is left, this is a sign that the soil is perfect for construction. But if the soil absorbs all the water in an hour or less or becomes all cracked up, it means that it's either too loose or too clay-like; this indicates that the land isn't ideal for construction. The second test involves digging a hole with the same afore-mentioned dimensions and then refilling it. If you refill the hole completely, whether you end up with excess soil or not, then the location is suitable for construction. But if you run out of the soil before refilling the hole completely, this suggests that the soil is too dense and holds excess moisture easily.

Site Orientation

According to the Vastu Purusha Mandala, designing spaces is easier when the orientation of the site itself is optimal. However, in Vastu Shastra, there is no particularly "evil" or "auspicious" direction; it all depends on the purpose of the building. Sites that face Purva (east) are best suited for schools and universities, as this direction provides enlightenment, making it the best for those constantly pursuing knowledge. Spots that face Uttara (north) are ideal for governmental buildings or any other structures reserved for those in positions of power, such as presidents, ministers, or congresspeople. But Dakshina-facing (south-facing) locations are usually used for commercial businesses. Finally, sites facing (west) are left for facilities that supply people with miscellaneous services. Buildings established in locations facing the cardinal directions recognized by Vastu Shastra will provide the people living or working in them with the benefits of being in sync with the natural elements. For architects, it is crucial to choose the right location when establishing residential or commercial buildings to make sure that the site itself is Vastu-compliant.

Location

The location of any property, whether residential or commercial, is the first thing you should be concerned about when you're on the market for one. Ideally, go for plenty of lush greenery areas, as this is a sign of prosperity. Never overlook the history of the property;

violence often leaves an imprint, so avoid properties sold by people in distress because the negative energy they've left behind will be transferred to you, causing you to be constantly on edge and ready to pick arguments. Properties, where people committed suicide or homicide are also a big no-no. You don't want to risk dealing with the negative imprint such tragic events leave in their wake.

If you're looking for a house, make sure that it's in a residential area. Living close to public places, such as schools, hospitals, and temples, goes against the rules of Vastu Shastra. Don't buy plots of land relatively smaller compared to the ones near it. Unconsciously, you might feel like you are less fortunate than your neighbors if you choose such a property setup. Properties blocked from the eastern direction by larger buildings are also considered inauspicious, as they get little natural sunlight. The same applies to habitations that have power supply stations in the northeastern direction. These stations create an "obstruction," which blocks the flow of positive energy and permeates the place with negative vibes.

In parallel, you must also be careful about the roads surrounding the property. Plots of land that face roads in the northeast are considered auspicious because this means that the northern part of the property is open, which is an important rule in Vastu Shastra. Finally, steer away from buildings or plots of land that face Y or T intersections (Veedi Shoolas). Veedi Shoolas draw negative energy, dust, and wind to the place, plus they considerably undermine your privacy. But if you've come across a great property that faces a Veedi Shoola, you can still make tweaks that will help you deflect the negative energy emanating from the intersection. For example, you can turn the part facing the road into a garage or a parking area. Using big trees or convex mirrors to block the intersection's negative energy is also an effective solution. If all fails, you can fence off that area. In any case, follow your intuition. If the place feels uncomfortable, simply continue your search for another property. Don't brush aside these feelings as pure superstition, as your body and soul know when they're not in sync with the elements. It's important to heed their warning.

Quick Vastu-Compliant Interior Design Tips

So, you've made sure that the location of your building and its orientation is Vastu-compliant, now what? Of course, it's time to tweak your interior design! Here's how you can follow Vastu Shastra's principles and ensure that your property retains its modern vibe:

• The main entrance of the building should face east or north and be made from high-quality wood. It should also open in a clockwise manner and be bigger than any other door the building has. Finally, don't paint it black or any other dark color or place garbage cans near it because this repels positive energy.

• If the building has a pooja or meditation room, use green and yellow for the walls and add incense sticks to repel negative energy. Avoid red because it indicates anger. Ideally, this room should face northeast or east.

• If a room includes electric appliances, they should be kept in the southwestern or western portion.

• Avoid including irregularly shaped furniture in any area, as it increases the flow of negative energy.

• Always keep the premises well-lit.

• Make sure that you're not facing any mirrors for extended periods. This entails removing mirrors placed in front of beds or couches. Mirrors are usually used to attract and lock in negative energy, protecting the place's residents from stumbling upon it. Although, staring too long in a mirror can make this energy reflect onto you. Also, avoid sitting with your back facing reflective surfaces.

• Remove any graffiti on the outside walls of the building, as it can bring chaos into your life if not tended to.

• Rooms where people congregate, such as living and meeting rooms, should be painted in yellow, white, blue, or green. Black and dark tones should generally be avoided.

• Colors like peach, pink, light green, blue, and orange can be used for cafeterias, dining rooms, and restaurants.

• Spaces that include the element of fire, such as kitchens, should be painted in fiery red, bright yellow, or orange to pay homage to Agni, the god of fire. Steer clear of dark tones to reduce the flow of negative energy, and shades of blue, because it's the color of the god of water, Varuna.

• Rest areas, including bedrooms and break rooms, can be painted in either blue and green for relaxation or brown for stability. If you and your partner recently got married, you can use colors like red and light pink to signify passion and intimacy. To increase productivity, you can try incorporating orange into the design of the room. Be careful, though, since people can get quickly agitated because of this color!

As we've seen, incorporating Vastu Shastra's principles in modern architecture and interior design isn't as complex as it sounds. While you may think that you must sacrifice the modern ambiance of your property to apply Vastu's teachings. I hope you now know how easy it is. Most important, don't listen to those who try to undersell Vastu Shastra as an outdated concept. This science is *very much* alive and well!

Chapter 8: Integrating Trees and Gardens

As you know by now, trees, plants, and plants make up a large part of Vastu practices. To put together a new garden, you can use the Vastu tips for gardening. Designing a garden from scratch can be an arduous task, as it will require guidance, planning, and consulting with experts to get the best results. Luckily, traditional Vastu guides for planting trees and designing gardens will alleviate that confusion and considerably facilitate this green endeavor. In this chapter, we'll explain how you can employ Vastu Shastra to create the perfect garden and breathe life into your house so positive energies keep flowing in.

Why are Trees and Plants Important Parts of Vastu?

Generally, the purpose of using Vastu to design your garden is to not only to offer a relaxing and positive environment but also to promote stability and the balance of energies inside and outside your house. Vastu Shastra highlights the importance of plants and greenery, as they're a symbol and embodiment of life. Their placement in the home can help instill serenity and happiness. If you notice that your premise lacks these elements, or if you sense an imbalance in your environment, plant more trees and potted plants. The Vastu charts will clearly show you which types of trees and plants to grow and where you can do that in compliance with auspicious directions.

Choose the Right Location

The first step to consider is the potential location for your new plants. According to Vastu's precepts, five elements exist in your garden, which you must remember for optimal plant and tree placement. While the southwest part of your house represents the earth element, the southeast section stands for fire and is ideal for disease-free plants. The northeast section is a symbol for water, while the northwest represents air. Finally, the center indicates the element of space. Each section will have a different bearing on this area, so plants should be planted according to the garden's location.

East-Facing Houses

Nothing in the Vastu guides indicates that you shouldn't plant trees in an east-facing house. Although, many homeowners have reported this can be considered a bad practice. It's preferable to plant trees on the west side instead; if that's unavoidable, you can create a water sump between the trees and your house to isolate the elements.

West-Facing Houses

If your house faces west, then you're in luck! This orientation is suitable for planting bigger trees. According to Vastu practices, this should avert predicaments and difficult situations for the home's occupants. Strong trees on the west side should help you feel secure and promote success. It should also make your identity more visible, which will help your social life prosper beyond measure.

North-Facing House

Unlike the west, the north direction isn't ideal for massive trees, as this might have adverse effects. Instead, you can choose gardening and planting more compact trees, such as bushes or shrubs. Flowerpots and smaller plants should work in your favor.

South-Facing House

Much like the western direction, the south is an ideal orientation to plant trees and heavy and dense plants. This will have a positive impact on both your health and wealth, as these elements will gravitate toward heavy trees in these areas.

Northeast-Facing House

Since the northeast is associated with a water element, heavy trees (or any tree), it won't be the best option for a garden facing that direction. Ideally, instead opt for grass, small plants, flowers, etc. for landscaping. In that direction, trees' added weight will have a negative effect and should be balanced out with a water sump, as recommended earlier.

Southeast-Facing House

The southeast is another optimal orientation for large and strong trees. If your home is along an east or southeast-facing road, a tree-lined road will dispel negative energies. This will ward off some of the adverse effects from the southwest direction, such as lack of income, bad reputation, and children disputes and rivalries in the household.

Northwest-Facing House

While this direction serves as the element of air, it can be an excellent direction for planting trees. However, to dissipate negative influences, your house's main door must face that direction. This should also be coupled with a naked wall for the home's exterior entrance and ensuring that the number of doors and windows is even.

Southwest-Facing House

Last, since the south and east directions are ideal for placing heavy, bushy trees, planting these same trees in a southwest-facing house is also encouraged. Tall trees in that direction will bring stability and promote a sense of strength. However, fruit-bearing trees are better planted on east-facing houses.

Garden Directions

Helped by these Vastu principles, you'll be able to outfit a beautiful garden from scratch. Before taking on this task, be careful when placing different elements in your garden to repel adverse energy and their spiritually harmful effects. For example, flowerbeds, decorative plants, and lawns should be placed on the garden's north and east sides. Also, to install a cascade or a water feature in your garden, make sure that it faces north or south since water is the element represented by the northeastern direction.

House Garden Trees and Plants

You can now select the types of trees to plant around your house according to your house direction. Now, before you do that, you must grow your knowledge on which types of trees and plants are the most suitable and highly regarded by Vastu practitioners. Here are the most common trees and plants used in Vastu Shastra practices and where to place them, along with their ideal placements:

Lucky Bamboo Plants

The Lucky Bamboo (scientific name Dracaena braunii) is one of the best plants to have in your garden, as it will attract peace and luck. It should promote health and increase wealth. Be sure not to mistake the Lucky Bamboo with the common bamboo plant, as both vary in shape, size, and effects. Also, avoid the Bonsai and the potted dwarf bamboos, as these are considered going against nature according to Vastu's practices. Lucky Bamboo plants must have a yellow bark instead of a dark-colored one.

Holy Basil Plants

This plant is amongst the best greeneries you can use in your garden. It is highly revered thanks to the positive energy it will bring to your premises. Ideally, it should grow in the north, east, or northeast directions. Also known as Tulsi, the Holy Basil plant is known for bringing auspiciousness and prosperity. As such, it must be used in the right direction to help you reap its benefits.

Flowerpots

While you may be tempted to place flowerpots just about everywhere, flower pots found on the wall, in the east, north, or northeast direction, will effectively block morning sunlight. Even when you feel sunlight coming from these directions, you won't enjoy its full benefits. Instead, you can place flowerpots or any decorative plants on the ground in these directions. Also, remember that they shouldn't grow taller than three feet.

Money Plants

Much like the Lucky Bamboo, the money plant (Epipremnum aureum) is a great source of luck and prosperity. Should you use these plants around your garden, you'll notice a significant increase in your wealth and quality of life. Therefore, you should be mindful of placing these plants to channel their positive effects. For instance, you can place pots of money plants either in the north or east direction, and avoid the south and west orientation.

Ashoka Trees

Ashoka trees, also known as Saraca Indica, should be placed in the south, east, or southeast direction as they are believed to bring joy and mitigate common aches and pain. Planting them in an auspicious direction should magnify these effects. Coconut trees (Cocos nucifera) will have a similar effect, which means you can safely use these trees with the Saraca Indica variety.

Banana Trees

Vastu advocates for planting banana trees in the northeast direction of the house. Also called Musa Genus, these trees enhance physical health and boost mental wellbeing. They also signify peace and serenity. People will even worship this tree, as it is considered sacred.

Mango Trees

Besides their medicinal properties, the leaves of the mango tree are commonly used as pesticides. The twigs can even be used for brushing your teeth. They are highly appreciated from a Vastu viewpoint, so they will be a nice addition to your garden. Plant these trees anywhere but the east or north directions to ward off the adverse and potentially health-damaging effects. Instead, you can plant them in the west direction.

Peonies

Peony flowers are colorful, beautiful, and deeply valued in Vastu practices. They're considered some of the most auspicious flowers and are commonly used in Hindi religious rituals and celebrations. Peonies are also a symbol of feminism and beauty. With their pleasant nature, a lot of Vastu practitioners plant these flowers in their gardens, ideally in the southwest direction.

Plum Blossoms

To invite harmony, wealth, and positive energy into your home, grow plum blossoms (Prunus Mume) in your garden. They're quite eye-pleasing and will promote positive energy all around. These flowers should be placed in the north or northeast direction. But many people believe that their orientation doesn't matter and suggest planting them where you see fit.

Dwarf Jade Plant

Like the spiritual properties of plum blossoms, dwarf jade plants (scientific name Portulacaria Afra) are great sources of positive energy and emit it around the house in abundance. This plant is also believed to attract luck, as it has five leaves, which symbolize the five elements of nature, or "Paanchbhootas." To place these plants in your garden, the north or east direction would be ideal.

Neem Trees

Finally, the Neem tree (Azadirachta Indica) is well known for its medicinal properties and is widely used in traditional holistic healing. Neem trees are also highly regarded in Vastu principles, as they are believed to be one of the most auspicious greeneries in any garden. Many people appreciate the natural flow of air that passes through neem trees directly into their living rooms or bedrooms for therapeutic and a refreshing aroma. Favor placing these trees in a northwest direction.

Roof Gardens and Indoor Plants

The same rules and precepts apply for designing a roof garden. Provided that the plot direction is Vastu-compliant, you can add potted plants and flowers as encouraged by Vastu placement principles. As far as indoor plants, you can use potted Lucky Bamboo plants, money plants, citrus plants, and lavender plants varieties, which will emanate organic, pleasant, and soothing scents in your entire house.

Balconies

Usually Vastu practitioners recommend using small potted plants. Compact and colorful plants should bring plenty of positive energy and allow it to flow about, especially in the right placement. Steer clear of large plants (like creepers) with a tendency to block sunlight effectively, drawing in negative energy and tipping the balance of spiritual influence in your home. Pots will also yield better effects when placed in the west, south, or southwest part of your balcony. Just be sure not to place them at the center to avoid obstructing the flow of energy.

Tips and Tricks

Now that you know more about the varieties of Vast-friendly trees and plants for your home, you're ready to move on to other types of plantations. Your garden can be a collection of shrubs, trees, and flowers that don't aren't mentioned in Vastu teachings. For this, you must know how to place them correctly for them not to interfere with the energy flow and positive effects of other elements in your garden. Here are a couple of useful tips you can follow:

If you're planting shrubs, make sure that they're well placed in the north or east sections of your garden.

Large trees shouldn't be placed too close to your house. The roots of large trees, such as peepal (ficus), can cause irreparable damages to your property. They can also attract rodents, insects, honeybees, etc., which should be avoided since they're considered bad omens.

Tall trees are to be placed in the south, west, and southwest direction of the garden. Likewise, they should also be kept a good distance away from your house to avoid bad luck and negative influences. According to Vastu Shastra principles, their shades should fall on the house between 9 AM and 3 PM.

Avoid thorny plants, like cactus or rose bushes, as they will give off negative energy, which will hinder your garden's positive influences.

Your lawn should be facing north or east. According to Vastu Shastra, a lawn with a swing with a north-south axis will provide multiple opportunities and favorable prospects.

If you're thinking about having a small waterfall installed, it should be placed in the north or east corner directions. Stay clear of the north-east orientation, as misplaced waterfalls or water features can cripple the peace and prosperity of your garden. You may also add a miniature pond with floating lotuses to promote good fortune.

Things to Avoid

There are certain things you must steer clear of to optimize your green space and garner the full benefits of Vastu Shastra. For example, thorny plants, can do more harm than good. They can weaken relationships, increase tension, and trigger fights. Bonsai plants are short, and will encourage stunted growth, either in fortune, career, or relationship matters.

As much as bamboo can be beneficial, it should be kept a fair distance from your house to achieve the best results. Neem trees must also be planted at least 60 meters away from your home. You must avoid adding any item that can inspire tension or violence in your garden, such as a scarecrow, as it will desecrate the peacefulness and serenity you've worked so hard to achieve.

Ultimately, constructing a Vastu-compliant garden can prove a challenging undertaking, especially if you don't have a specific set of instructions or aren't sure of where to start. The best way to tackle this is to take one step at a time, know which direction your home is facing, and then decide which varieties of trees, plants, and flowers you'd like to plant in your garden. It's worth mentioning that, in some scenarios, you might have to remove already-existing elements in your garden to achieve optimum results.

Chapter 9: Pyramids: The Mystery of Energy Concentration

A cornerstone of Vastu Shastra is the pyramid. To understand how it works, one must first go back to Vastu fundamentals. As you now know, Vastu relies on science and the universe's spiritual energy, effectively merging and elevating these two areas of knowledge. Energy channels substance towards the spirit and life, helping them live purposefully and prosperously. Despite being negative this energy creates all that we see in our daily lives and can be centered on the pyramid where it resonates and permeates living beings.

Of Greek origin, the word "pyra" means fire, and "mid" means energy, which explains why the pyramid holds such a strong meaning in Vastu philosophy. The term "pyramid" also denotes a geometrical object which has sides that join at an apex point. Due to the powerful energy that resonates with their unique structures, pyramids are considered powerful objects, which explains why the ancient Egyptians were so keen on using them to build tombs and put life to rest. Energy feeds life into us, and perhaps that was what they were attempting to achieve.

How the Pyramid Works

Typically, there are two rules to how the pyramid works with Vastu Shastra. The one dictates that the energy is highly concentrated around the axis that travels across the pyramid. The second rule holds that the energy is channeled out of the apex of the pyramid. This phenomenon affects all lives and humans and impacts any location's energy levels, helping buildings and homes strike a positive and nurturing balance. This concept is related to bio-geometry, a branch of science that focuses on the study of structures, like pyramids, their dimensions, and their effects on living organisms, particularly humans. For example, conical, square, and pyramidal patterns will all have various bearings on human bodies or living organisms. Incidentally, how energy is channeled in Vastu Shastra differs from how it is used in Feng Shui, as both have their own approaches and methods for funneling energies.

How They Can Be Used

In Vastu, the pyramid can be a pivotal center of energy in your house and possibly your entire existence. Therefore, countless people use it for blocking negative energy and drawing in the more positive influences. To unlock the secrets of this iconic instrument for your home, here are several useful pointers:

Thanks to their effectiveness in dispelling negative energies, Vastu pyramids are used in homes, especially at the corner of the house, for an optimal effect.

If you have an impaired energy flow in a certain room, you can reenergize that space by adding Vastu pyramids to all four corners. Once you're done with that step, you'll notice a sense of coordination and positivity taking effect in the room.

If you're concerned about energy levels in the workspace, particularly in your office, you can place one pyramid on your desk. Aside from acting as a nice décor item, you'll soon notice a more positive and conducive ambiance.

Due to their ability to channel large quantities of energy in any space, you can carry on with your meditative practices under one pyramid. This should help strengthen your mental faculties, concentration, and boost your meditation experience at once.

Vastu pyramids can also be kept underwater to support the positive energy flow across your metabolic water balance. If you experience digestion issues or stomach aches, placing Vastu pyramids underwater will help you.

Like the above, the Vastu pyramid can preserve your food items or any products you possess for a substantial amount of time.

Placement

Following the placement and directions of Vastu guides can appear a daunting task, especially for novices. Luckily, the Vastu pyramid placement isn't as difficult as following other, more complex Vastu precepts. They can either be placed in a central point, at the corners, or any location in which energy is most prominent. You can also place them in your bedroom, office, car, or simply even in your pocket.

The Various Types of the Vastu Pyramid

While they essentially share the same shape, Vastu pyramids can vary in quality, material, and size. You have the liberty to choose whichever type of Vastu pyramid appeals to you the most, as they will all serve the purpose of purifying and concentrating positive energy in your surroundings. However, it never hurts to learn more about the Vastu pyramid's different iterations, along with their unique characteristics and properties.

Promax Pyramids

These pyramids are known for their power to produce large quantities of energies through their nine-layer energy grid. The Promax top and gold plate are located at the sides and both channel energy; they are supported by an energy plate at the bottom of the pyramid. They're generally used when working on the land, building construction, financial and investment operations, and miscellaneous projects. So, use this pyramid on these premises.

Flat Max Pyramids

As the name suggests, these pyramids are flat and are specifically designed for apartments. By using one pyramid in your flat, it'll help you magnify energy concentrations, which will instantly increase the flow of positive energies and boost your home's spiritual value. This may include better energy balance, wealth, and a more prosperous lifestyle. You can also use these pyramids in shops, factories, or large family homes.

Agro Pyramid

If you're struggling to grow your garden, agro pyramids will be the most suitable solution in this scenario. Agro pyramids foster an immense, mystical power that can influence the growth and distribution of good grain with little effort. They should also improve the quality of your greenery, vegetables, fruits, and herbs, so you can use them in your garden for that purpose.

Super Max Pyramids

As mentioned earlier, pyramids will have similar effects in cleansing your location of negative energies and concentrating on the positive ones. In that regard, many Vastu practitioners claim that supermax pyramids will have an even greater magnifying effect. They're ideal in situations where the energy balance is leaning towards the negative side. These pyramids usually have a gold center, which explains why you're bound to experience an exponential increase in energy. These can be used anywhere, but they're more prevalent in homes and offices. Supermax pyramids can also increase your wealth and health, so they're one of the best Vastu pyramids you can decorate your space with.

Multi-Tier 9 x 9 Pyramid

The multi-tier 9 x 9 pyramid is known for its Vastu and Feng Shui curative properties. It's mostly used in Vastu remedies to optimize energy balance and is also capable of land charging and activating the room's center. Most of the multi-tier 9 x 9 pyramids contain neutron polymers to achieve effective and immediate results once the pyramid is used. It's also made up of a pyra top, a pyra plate, and nine pyra chips, which are fixed to the base of the pyramid with adhesive material. Depending on your needs and the space's configuration, you can place that pyramid on the ground, on a desk, attach it to your ceiling, or fix it to a wall.

Bemor 9 x 9 Pyramid

If you're looking for a Vastu-approved apparatus to enhance your luck (aside from arranging your house according to the favored direction), Bemor 9 x 9 pyramids should be your go-to choice. These pyramids improve their users' luck and energize their homes, much like the other pyramids listed here. These pyramids will often be found around office spaces, where they can increase wealth and income, and homes to attract and hoard the much-needed positive energy. Bemor pyramids come with nine pyra chips, one pyra plate, and a lotus power hole plate.

Which Material to Opt For

As you may already know, the first built pyramids were made from rock stones, but now, there are several options you can choose from, from rare metals to ordinary plastic. Before you decide which material to select, you must decide the purpose of the activity you'll be using the pyramid for. For instance, if you will use it for yoga, concentration, or any meditative activity, your ideal choice will be stone. But plastic or glass pyramids are better suited for energy magnification, yet must be kept in bright, well-lit locations.

In parallel, crystal pyramids won't only embrace the positive energy, but they'll also prevent negativity from entering your house. Pyramids made of this precious material are also ideal for healing sickness, improving mental faculties, enhancing your intuition, and even losing weight. This will depend on the crystal you're using, though. For example, agate will have a significant calming effect. Bloodstone will promote good blood circulation and cardiovascular health. Moonstone is more appropriate for the ladies, as it works on improving feminine health. Clear quartz is ideal for meditative activities. Finally, snowflake obsidian will help boost your immune system. If you will use crystal pyramids, make sure that you have four to be placed at each corner of the room to reap maximum benefits.

Benefits of Vastu Pyramids

By now, you may have guessed that the main purpose of Vastu pyramids is to direct positive energy towards you and your house. However, the benefits you will garner from these powerful items will build up eventually. After a few months of using Vastu pyramids, you'll notice tremendous changes in your life. The following outlines the changes you'll most likely experience.

Wealth and Prosperity

According to Vastu precepts, the idea according to which money can't buy happiness is null. Vastu Shastra acknowledges that it can indeed affect our lives. This is why most of Vastu's practices harness cosmic energy to bring wealth and financial prosperity to their users. Within months of using Vastu pyramids, be it in your office or at your house, you'll notice that both your fortune and income will have increased, which will help you enjoy a better lifestyle for both you and your family.

Love Life

Many people struggle with their personal relationships for years on end. Some will even think that they'll never meet their soulmate or find true love. Using Vastu pyramids can alter your perspective. Once the right placement of the pyramids is achieved, positive energies will attract a potential companion who brings happiness and harmony into your life. If marriage is your goal, then you're bound to have a happy and long-lasting one when using a Vastu pyramid.

Family

Vastu pyramids can affect our relationships with our entourage. To build a loving, harmonious family, adding the right Vastu pyramids to your home will get you closer to that aspiration. Remember, though, that you should at least be familiar with Vastu practices for this to work. As discussed in the previous chapter, thorny plants in your garden (cactus, roses) can interfere with the energies emitted by the pyramids, hence the importance of strategic placement. Family plays a central role in our lives, so you must follow Vastu's recommendations to the letter to nurture peaceful and cordial relationships with your loved ones.

Health

Invariably, pyramids are most often used to improve one's health. Few things can stop you from making progress as much as impaired health, be it in your work, relationships, or your meditation goals. Pyramids work to negative energies and their damaging effects. By using the right type and number of pyramids, you'll be able to maintain a disease-free environment and protect your home's occupants from illness and health-related conditions.

Education

Education is a quintessential aspect of your children's lives. To see your children grow to their fullest potential, you must give them the best education you can afford as any caring parent would. While Vastu pyramids won't have a direct hand in this, they can always bring your children positive and rewarding opportunities for their development. They'll improve their cognitive functions, concentration, and overall health, all of which will promise them to stellar education and career.

Protection and Purification

As established, one objective of Vastu Shastra is to dispel any evil or negative energy from your living and working environment. Pyramids can serve as a potent source of protection against this devilry. They should also take instant effect once you place them correctly around your space. You can also place Vastu pyramids in your car to make sure your safety and that of all passengers.

Other Vastu Tools

While diverting your interest in Vastu pyramids, you mustn't neglect to combine them with other tools to optimize the pooling of positive energies in your home. For instance, Vastu sleep is a useful tool you can keep under your mattress. Its purpose is to garner the benefits of cosmic energies and improve the quality of your sleep. If your mind is often troubled, and you find yourself prone to chronic insomnia, you can use Vastu sleep to soothe your body, spirit, and mind. It should also work in harmony with pyramids placed in your bedroom to foster success, enhance your health, and promote serenity.

Another instrument you can use with the pyramids is the pyra cap. Pyra caps are basically pyramid-shaped accessories you can wear on your head during your meditation sessions. They're said to improve mind power during meditation, especially when the practice is conducted under a pyramid. Acquiring a pyra cap is a must if you're channeling Vastu Shastra for meditation or yoga. Pyra caps improve concentration and confidence. They can also help your mind relax and alleviate stress without you having to take any medication. To reap the full benefits of a meditation session, you should use a pyra cap.

Pyramid Roof

While pyramid roofs are not technically considered Vastu pyramids, people have reported these roofs carry surprising effectiveness. It's also recommended that you create a pyramid roof for your living room if it's the central part of your house, which it generally is. Sitting under a pyramid roof will positively influence your memory power, reduce backaches, headaches, and be a remedy to your insomnia. If you're going to place pyramids in other parts of your house, make sure that one of the triangles faces north. This should also be the case for your pyramid roof; in fact, pyramid roofs can have an even more powerful effect than small-sized pyramids and will work in harmony with other pyramidal structures placed in the corners of your house.

All in all, Vastu pyramids are essential for any Vastu practitioner. Given how easy it is to use them, you won't have to deal with the confusion of directions and orientations often associated with Vastu. Fortunately, these pyramids come in all shapes and sizes, and each type boasts its own unique properties and set of benefits. To ensure you get the best Vastu pyramid for your house or workspace, you must document yourself further to decide which one would be ideal according to your needs and aspirations. The energy that comes from these pyramids is primordial for humans, living beings, and our planet, so it's only fair it must be channeled correctly and purified from any negative, potentially noxious influences.

Chapter 10: Destructive Vastu Remedies

The ideal way to build a home or a workplace that abides by the majority of Vastu principles is by making sure that they're implemented right from the beginning of the conception and building phase. Now, since not many people know the Vastu concepts or aren't convinced of their effects and benefits early on, this aspect is largely overlooked. Fortunately, it's possible to instill the right energy and frequency, even if your home or workplace wasn't built according to the precepts of Vastu Shastra. While this chapter's name has nothing to do with actual destruction or ruin, it is rather about rebuilding and renovation to resolve a challenging situation through the effective use and implementation of Vastu principles.

Considerations Before Applying the Principles

When you start putting what you've learned from Vastu Shastra into practice, you'll notice that it can be quite flexible. There are no hard or rigid rules that will prevent you from inviting harmony and prosperity into your home or workplace the way you see it. Vastu science sees a building or space as a living organism, making it possible to approach it from different perspectives. Achieving even half of the principles of Vastu is considered a job well done. It's important to perceive the space that you're trying to build or decorate as an integral part of yourself, intact with your frequency and vibrations. By respecting the laws of nature, you're ensuring that the space is harmoniously balanced, which is why it shouldn't be tackled as yet another tedious renovation job.

One of the most important considerations to factor into this process is the individuals' unique characteristics and personalities in a workspace or home. You shouldn't think of the space as your own because if other people spend a lot of time in it, their thoughts and needs are bound to be an element of consideration in any Vastu remedy. Think of your space as a temple that deeply nurtures your spirit and soul; building it properly becomes primordial to make sure that your spirituality and internal energy balance are prosperous and well-guarded.

No matter how one tries to put it, the physical space you spend most of your time in will necessarily affect you in a variety of ways, for better or worse. This is why Vastu principles are highly sought after, namely, to ensure that the effects always tip towards the positive side. You may need to take a moment to analyze yourself, your lifestyle, and your needs, to discover a pattern that can make sure your personal comfort and convenience.

Proceeding with Care

When you use destructive Vastu remedies, it's always important to be careful about the changes you're planning. As explained, buildings and their surroundings should be treated as organisms that foster fluctuating energies. Modifying a space too much and in the wrong direction can hinder the vibrations and energy of the place, ultimately disrupting your own harmony and spiritual balance. It's best to draw a design copy of the alterations you want to make and use a Vastu blueprint that incorporates the five elements to tell whether your modifications would be harming any of them, albeit slightly. Fire and water elements are often the most clashing elements in many setups, especially those in the kitchen (faucets, ovens, etc.).

Invariably, there are several drawbacks to a kitchen that doesn't follow The Vastu principles. If you enjoy cooking and spending a lot of time in your home kitchen, you might be putting a lot at stake if you choose not to follow the Vastu guidelines. Chronic conditions and inexplicable diseases can affect the house chef if the cooking space is teeming with malicious vibrations caused by inauspicious furniture and hardware placement, along with an inadequate orientation of the kitchen. There is also the possibility of arising family problems, which can upset even the strongest of relationships.

How to Redesign your Kitchen

Since the kitchen is one of the core areas of any house, using destructive Vastu remedies can effectively help cleanse it of any bad energy.

The Placement of the Space

If you're still deciding where to place the kitchen, it's recommended to go for the southeast direction, where the fire element is dominant. If that's not feasible, you can also choose a northwest orientation.

Placement of Stove and Sink

Align your stove in the southeast direction to establish that the person using it is always facing east. In parallel, make sure that the sinks and taps are placed on the opposite side of the stove, as water and fire elements should never mingle. The flowing of the water should abide by a northeast direction to promote positive and rewarding energies.

Placement of the Refrigerator

Try to find a location for the refrigerator that isn't in the northeast direction. Avoid placing it in a corner. Generally, you should place no electrical appliances in the northeast direction of the kitchen.

Placement of Storage and Water Vessels

You can choose either the western or eastern side of your space for storage. For the water vessels, you'll want to go toward water, which should be on the northeastern side of your kitchen.

Design and Colors

Suppose you're in the right state of energy to renovate your kitchen and make it Vastu-compliant. In that case, favor ceramic tiles or marble material for the floorings because of their durability and consistency. Adding a few colors may be overlooked by many people, but this is an essential element in any space's energy optimization process. In the southeast corner of your kitchen, try adding hues of soft red. If you're handling the kitchen flooring, best to go with white, off-white, creamy, or light gray colors to give it a solid look and grounded feel. Also, please go for expressive colors like red, yellow, orange, or purple for the décor. You can rarely go wrong with most colors in the kitchen, to the exception of black, which you should avoid because of the negative energy it can harbor.

Leveraging Vastu to Prevent Theft

One of Vastu designs' many benefits is its proven effect in controlling external factors that can hinder your well-being. Theft is one of the most common ailments that can plague a non-Vastu-compliant home. This doesn't mean that Vastu will prevent all types of theft as if it were a steel gate, but it can keep a lot of problems at bay when you address it early on. The location of the door, its direction, the material it's made of, and many factors are features in the Vastu practice to help avert the incidence of thefts.

If you own valuables like jewelry or cash that you'd like to keep in the house, avoid placing it on the northwest side since it can increase instructions and break-ins.

Always make sure that the main entrance to your home is noticeably bigger than any other door in your house.

If you have multiple doors and windows, make sure that their number is an even number.

Use sacred symbols as decorations beside the entrance doors.

Obstructions to the house's main entrance should be removed because they disrupt the energy flow both inside and outside the house.

Avoid photographs, posters, or art that portray a malicious or evil aura (scenes of horror, violence, or despair) as this can bring in noxious energies.

Understanding the Necessity of Demolitions

Many people are reluctant to destroying a piece of their property, even when they know it can be for the best. Most Vastu consultants will try their best to work out a way to avoid demolition, but when that's inexorable, some extra work is due. One dilemma you might face, for example, is a toilet or staircase in the northeast direction. While Feng Shui may offer solutions to alleviate the negative energy through certain items, it won't be more than a temporary solution; removing these structures is sometimes the only remedy.

If you plan on applying Vastu principles to the letter, you must let go of any reluctance you may have about destructive remedies. If a structure is causing a clash with Vastu tenets in the house, you must remove it. Not that it's the only way, but you need to be mentally prepared for worst-case scenarios.

Dealing with Wells and Extensions

If you live in a house with a well in the property's southeast direction, you might need to remove it or bury it with mud or stone. Many people use lids to close the wells, but this isn't the most effective way. Permanent solutions are the best way to deal with these structures to avoid future, potentially costly hassles.

Extensions leaning towards the northwest section in a property are notoriously difficult to resolve without using destructive Vastu remedies. You can start by adjusting the boundaries of that extension or implementing a doorway to delimit a northeastern corner to mitigate that direction's effect. You may be tempted to place idols instead of doing this, but that will only temporarily solve a part of the problem.

Painting the Walls

Depending on the state of your interior walls, a paint job can be considered both a destructive and non-destructive Vastu remedy. You cannot randomly paint the walls hoping for harmonious results. You need to consider the room you are painting to ensure compliance with the Vastu principles.

Living Room

The living room is a very important section of your house and is usually the first your visitors are introduced to. As such, you'll want to make it look bold and lively by using warm and energetic colors like blue, yellow, off-white, and green. Add a hint of red for an added energy boost, but in moderation.

Dining Room

The dining room's colors should reflect good health and prosperity, so choosing relaxing colors that can put you in a state of ease is highly recommended. Blue, pink, and green are all viable options you can paint the walls with for the most tranquil and soothing effect.

Master Bedroom

The bedroom should always induce a sense of relaxation, besides little hints of romantic vitality. The most favored colors are blue, pink, or purple. Avoid darker shades of these colors to maintain a tranquil and effective color scheme.

Guest Bedroom

The guest bedroom is generally designed for temporary stays, which means you can offer more than the usual relaxing colors by choosing light shades of yellow, orange, or lavender. These colors can exude a royal sense of belonging and intimacy to your visiting guests.

Study or Work Room

For this space, you'll want to select colors that promote concentration, and according to Vastu, those would be green, blue, and purple in their lightest shades to avoid distractions and loss of focus. This should help make the environment comfortable and pleasant enough to boost your productivity and mental faculties.

Bathroom

People always consider their bathroom to be the most private and even the safest space around their homes. It should always give off relaxing vibrations. The colors you should use for these rooms should be dark shades of black, gray, white, pink, or a mix of them all. Elegance and comfort should be combined to secure that your bathroom is aesthetically pleasing and conducive to a good energy balance.

Renovations in the Bedroom

Whatever you're trying to achieve, avoid having a bedroom in the southeast direction. According to the most basic Vastu precepts, these rooms should be in almost any corner except the southeastern one. If you already have a bedroom in there, relocate it all together. As a temporary solution, you can shift the bed away from the room's corner to avoid the fire vibrations in this quadrant. If you have a master bedroom with an adjacent bathroom, you'll want to make sure it's directed towards the east or north sides of the room. It's also essential to keep the attached bathroom door always closed, and to keep the toilet seat down. Because of Vastu principles, mirrors shouldn't be in the bedroom if you have a partner because they can lead to frequent fights and tense up the environment. However, if you find that a mirror is an essential item in your bedroom, then try to place it on the northeastern wall of the room.

Renovations in the Living Room

The living room is the heart of your house and its influence extends well beyond the walls that bind it. This signifies that having negative vibrations in the living room can resonate in other rooms as well. Idols, paintings, and other decorations are great additions, but they shouldn't be your main point of focus unless you make sure that the living room is properly Vastu-compliant first. Here are useful living room arrangement and renovations tips:

You can choose between the northwest, northeast, northern, and southwest directions if you're planning to move your living room. The perfect setup for those who don't like parties or having company over is usually the northwestern section of your house, as it belongs to the air quadrant, which depicts activity and movement. The southwestern location is ideal for get-togethers and late-night parties because visitors always prefer this direction. If you're looking to foster positive energy coupled with nature's calm tranquility, the northeastern location is a sure-fire option.

Assess if you can restructure the beams or girders on the ceiling because they can induce stress, a sense of heaviness, and inauspicious vibes.

If the living room entrance is in the southwestern corner, you might need to restructure the entrance to move it toward the western direction.

Vastu in the Office

If you're managing an office you must attend to countless details that can cause a myriad of issues if left unchecked. If your office is facing east, try shifting the balance towards the west because it brings strength, stability, and balance. Try to remove any office-related equipment from the northeastern section of the space and move the water resources over there. You may also need to relocate the staircase if it stands in the center of the office because it can disrupt energy flow. The reception should almost always be in the northeastern direction, which can be problematic if the staircase is in the space.

The majority of destructive Vastu remedies shouldn't be attempted solo if you have no experience in renovations or DIY projects. Your best bet is to solicit the services of a professional Vastu consultant to help guide you through the process, no matter how much work is required. Ultimately, tackling these issues is primordial if you're planning on transforming your house or office into a Vastu-compliant paradise.

Chapter 11: Non-Destructive Vastu Remedies

Understanding the science of Vastu Shastra enables you to eradicate any source of harmful energy in your building. Learning more about the balance and dynamics of energy gives you a chance to harness positive ones for your gains without having to destroy or demolish your surroundings. While the science of Vastu might revolve around directions, cosmic energies need to be considered as well. The energy emitted by your belongings (property, furniture, décor items) should not be neglected throughout your journey. Think of Vastu as a balance you can bring to your home or workspace with non-destructive remedies. The majority of Vastu experts believe that mental and physical impairments, mostly, result from ignoring Vastu principles. Neglecting the application of Vastu remedies in your living space can lead to financial issues, given how difficult it will be to contribute your best work. To help you in repelling bad energies and welcoming good vibes in your building, this chapter will delve into the characteristics and applications of non-destructive Vastu remedies.

Walls and Colors

In Vastu, walls are considered the foundation of any building; they represent support and strength. This is the first element to consider when you're trying to balance energies and fill your house with positivity. Since colors hold a lot of weight, they require proper attention and care. Even if you live in an already-finished home, it's easy to repaint the walls to foster good energy and prosperity. Color theory isn't just about matching colors on a wheel, but, it's a science you must delve into to select the right colors for the energies you wish to attract. Invariably, the aesthetic and palette you choose should align with your inner self; neglecting this aspect might make you feel out of place and detached from the place. It's imperative to consider Vastu principles and the color theory and choose the colors you feel connected with the most.

Warm, strong colors such as red represent passion, vibrancy, and liveliness. Given these attributes, you must be cautious with it. For example, your bedroom should never be painted in red because this will promote discomfort and make you angry and on edge. But red works great in living rooms as it suggests warmth and high energy. Yellow is another warm color that signifies boldness and courage. It emits feelings of warmth, elation, and optimism. While yellow is best used combined with other colors to elevate a room and make it appear larger, it's suitable for children's bedrooms. However, choose lighter or more faded shades of the color, like soft pastels.

Cold colors such as blue or green are more calming, soothing, and grounding. It's no wonder why blue has been regarded as the color of eternal beauty across time and cultures. It's the color of the sky and the sea that evokes tranquility and serenity. According to Vastu precepts, blue is more suited for large areas where you need peace and calmness. In parallel, green is one of the best cold colors for attracting wealth, stability, and promoting individual growth. When you repaint a wall in lime, sage, mint, or sea-foam, it changes the mood of the room and makes space become more soothing and welcoming.

Lighting

The late Martin Luther King Jr. famously once said that darkness could not drive out darkness; only light can do so. This quote is inspired by Hindu philosophy and its interest in studying different light sources, along with how the impact of their placement. Harnessing positive energies in your living or working space cannot be achieved without the right lighting. Let's explore how lighting can do wonders for your space with just a few simple changes:

Never ignore filling your space with good lighting; light can effectively transform any room's feel and atmosphere. Good lighting can have a positive, uplifting effect on your mood and mental state. So, always start by allowing a source of bright light, especially around your house's main door, to attract positivity and prosperity.

Make sure that the corners of every room are well lit. Not only will this illuminate your space and make it seem wider and more pleasant to the eye, but it also welcomes good vibes into your space.

Natural sunlight is key to balancing energies in your house, hence the importance of ensuring that your whole building, especially your home office or workplace, has constant access to natural light. This will provide warmth and stability to your space while bringing in vibes of joy and comfort that will boost your productivity and concentration.

The light emanating from fireplaces and candles is naturally soothing and relaxing and usually fit best in the living room, bathroom, and bedroom. This will elevate the mood of these rooms to transform them into peaceful and relaxing dens.

In Hindu philosophy, it's believed that the northeastern corner of any space is the Sattva corner, which represents one of the three essential modes of existence. The majority of Vastu experts also believe that allowing natural light to enter from this corner symbolizes creativity, positive energy, and wealth for the occupants. Negativity, on the other hand, is represented by the southwestern corner. As such, you must make sure that the main sources of lighting in any space is placed in the sattva corner.

Finally, your bathroom lighting shouldn't be overlooked, especially the ones surrounding the mirror. The light you need to add to this area should be diffused and not display any glares or shadows.

Vastu For Bedrooms

Many people don't find comfort in their own bedrooms when this should be their space for comfort and relaxation, which is always a demoralizing prospect. Without comfort in your bedroom, you'll be more likely to feel worn out and stressed. Applying the Vastu principles can prove highly beneficial for optimizing and harmonizing your bedroom for an unparalleled living and resting experience. Consider these useful pointers:

According to ancient Vastu beliefs, the southwest corner of the building is the ideal location for the bedroom as it's believed to attract longevity, health, and prosperity.

The northwest corner is more suitable for children or guest bedrooms. The northeast and southeast corners should be avoided as they're believed to increase physical health issues, mental health challenges, and household conflicts.

If you live in a house that already has bedrooms in its northeast or southeast corners, there are some non-destructive remedies to balance out the negative energies. For instance, you may use lavender essential oil or incense sticks to compensate for any structural defects your house might have. Another remedy you can safely use involves placing small bowls of coarse or sea salt in each corner of the room to fill it with good energy and repel any negative ones.

As per the Vastu tradition, your bed should ideally be placed in the southwest corner of the room. When sleeping, make sure that your head points to either the south or the east. Otherwise, this will prevent your body from absorbing positive and rejuvenating vibrations. But it's been established that a couple sharing a bed should always sleep with their heads towards the south and their legs pointing to the north.

Vastu principles dictate that the shape of your bed should be a rectangle or a square. Generally, it is best to steer clear of unconventional shapes for furniture pieces around the home. The most suitable material for your bed is wood, ideally the organic, non-recycled kind.

According to Vastu specialists, placing the bed under a beam or near a sidewall is a big no-no. However, you could always have a fake ceiling installed to avoid this common oversight. Also, make sure that there's enough room around it for you to access the bed easily from both sides.

Artwork and Plants

Paintings, artwork, and interior plants are an integral part of any culture and design philosophy. But people are questioning their painting choices, for foregoing artworks altogether for fear of selecting illustrations that might attract negative energies or evil forces. This habit stems from the confusion that many people experience when trying to choose pictures compliant with Vastu to complement their houses. Invariably, artwork and house plants are excellent choices for houses and buildings to promote growth and happy vibes and make the space beautiful and well put together. Here are a few tips to aid you in your search for auspicious decorative items that will bring your home together in harmony and unity.

If your living room has a southwest wall, make use of it to hang a family portrait with a bright spotlight that highlights the photo. This is believed to bring health, luck, and good fortune for the family members.

Avoid representations of violence, suffering, or death in your artwork. Instead, choose inspiring and visually pleasing subjects such as natural landscapes, exotic destinations, geometric patterns, or whatever strikes your fancy.

To harness positive energies and trap them into your house, bamboo plants will be your go-to for good luck. The most popular choice nowadays is the money plant, yet you need to be careful about its placement. As explained in a previous chapter, it should be placed in the southern or northern corner of the room to attract wealth and fortune. With plants, you can get creative if you choose positive colors you feel connected to. You can arrange different colorful flowers and plants such as purple orchids or plum blossoms that suggest positivity and wealth.

Some plants don't have a place inside in the house, including thorny plants like cacti because they're believed to attract negative energies and inauspiciousness. Also avoid plants that hamper growth, such as miniature bonsai trees. If you're a fan of big plants, best to avoid placing them in the northern corner of your space as they might hinder positive vibes.

Vastu-compliant decorative items aren't simply limited to paintings and plants. For example, adding a crystal chandelier to your living room can effectively attract good tidings to your space. However, balance it out with the other elements. You can also make use of candles with artful holders to impart aesthetics, warmth, and contentment in your living area.

Mirrors

Adding the right mirrors in terms of shape, placement, and size can be tricky to master. Adding mirrors plays a huge role in reflecting your whole house with positive vibes and expelling negative energy. Mirrors are also considered a quick fix for the removal of Vastu-related troubles. According to Vastu Shastra, there are three fundamental rules to observe for optimal mirror placement. The first rule is to never place a mirror facing the main door as it's said to harbor inauspiciousness and cause turbulence in the home. The second guideline dictates you shouldn't put up a mirror that directly faces your bed, as it can be a great source of harm and instability in the household. Finally, placing two mirrors in front of each other should also be avoided to prevent magnifying any bad energy that might be lurking around your space.

With a few simple tricks, you can attend to any Vastu shortcomings your house might be enduring. When applying these principles, the most important thing is to choose what best suits your personality and energy profile. When focusing on making your home Vastu-friendly, always be sure to select designs and dispositions that reflect your preferences. This will help you optimize the space in a unique, effortless, and harmonious fashion.

Chapter 12: Feng Shui Remedies for Harmonious Living

As we've learned early on, the term Feng Shui literally translates to "wind-water" and signifies a harmonious flow of energy. Feng Shui works in such a way that it's made many people believe it's a form of magic reserved for a privileged few with strong intuitive psychic powers. In reality, Feng Shui is merely but a philosophical system with well-defined rules and beliefs that can effectively transform any dwelling into a harmonious and united space filled with positive energy. Feng Shui is considered a science that takes both the Earth's and cosmic energies into account. While it might seem a complex and esoteric concept, much like Vastu Shastra, the trick is to avoid jumping right into its precepts without a proper understanding of its benefits and applications. You can start with simple yet effective remedies to turn your space into a healthy and harmonious environment that reflects positively on you and your family's mental state, physical health, and achievements in life. Let's see how you can achieve this delicate balance with ease.

Perfect Your Center Point

As with any design philosophy, it's crucial to pay attention to every detail that goes into forming your living space. According to Feng

Shui's principles, the center of your living space harbors the utmost gravity. This essentially means that, to balance out the different energies to achieve harmony, stability, and contentment, you must make sure that the heart of your home fosters spiritual nourishment and positive energy. The house's center is usually called the *Yin-Yang point*, where all opposites meet and blend with one another. This elemental point should look pleasing, feel comfortable, and have a coherent design to bring balance and harmony to your space. You may also place your favorite décor items at the center of your house to allow your spirit and soul to be surrounded by peace, beauty, and harmoniousness.

Aim for a More Welcoming Entry Path

Chi refers to the balance between Yin and Yang; it's the energy of life and the center around which the universe revolves. In Feng Shui, your home's exterior entrance leading to the main door is believed to be the opening of Chi. This is a gateway for positive energies that support growth, wealth, and fortune. As such, it's imperative to embellish your entry path by filling it with greenery and beautiful, soothing lights. You can also go the extra mile by adding an assortment of fragrant, dopamine-stimulating flowers. Likewise, add anything that makes you feel more energized, happy, and comforted, such as a collection of crystals, stress-relieving objects, small water fountains, illustrations, or chimes. Another thing to consider, according to Feng Shui, is that you and your family should make it a habit to always use your house's front door as the main entry gate. Using the back door can pave the way for negative and harmful energies to permeate your home.

Always Declutter

Cluttered spaces are often considered the root of all evil, especially in rooms where you're meant to be relaxing or getting work done. You can dedicate a few hours of your time every week to look around the house for anything you no longer have a use for, from shrunken clothes to worn-out furniture pieces and dysfunctional appliances. So, get rid of these items regularly to avoid pile-ups and non-optimal exploitation of your surface area. Cluttered spaces affect us on different levels consciously and subconsciously as they can increase stress levels and hinder wellbeing and productivity. It's also believed that a messy home promotes a wish to add more to your possessions until you end up becoming a compulsive hoarder. But material objects can never offer that level of satisfaction and fulfillment that most of us expect from buying clothes, electronics, and all those things that litter our interiors pointlessly.

Functionality is Essential

While the science and practice of Feng Shui are typically associated with spirituality and energy balance, there exists an indirect link between the flow of energy and the functionality of the objects found in any home. Postponing minor repairs or replacements might hamper the natural flow of Chi and make way for negative energies to proliferate in your space. You must always ensure that everything in your house is in order and functioning as it should. Fix jammed doors, change light bulbs, repair broken fans or air conditioning vents, attend to leaks, and even change batteries yourself if you can. Where possible, always mend the flaws yourself unless it's something you genuinely cannot do, such as HVAC, advanced electrics, plumbing, etc.

Leave Work Out of the Bedroom

In today's world, many people have resorted to remote or freelance work, either by choice or due to global circumstances. This has led many to develop the habit of working in bed or from their bedrooms' comfort. According to Feng Shui precepts, this is a big no-no. The bedroom should serve its purpose relaxation only, sleeping, and enjoyment. You should never invite energies of stress, impatience, and restlessness into your bedroom by turning it into a workstation. If you're working from home, dedicate a space in your living room or an entire room to turn into a work corner or home office. This will help establish healthy boundaries in your interior, which will bring stability and optimize all its occupants' wellbeing.

Harmonious Bedroom

Now that we've established one of the cardinal rules about the bedroom, the following helpful bedroom tips will promote harmony and unity within your sacred space:

Start by placing your bed in such a way it has a solid wall behind it. By doing this, you'll bring energies of stability and comfort your way. This is essential for proper, quality sleep. Applying this simple change will help you rest and recuperate faster and better, which works to boost your productivity and concentration levels during the daytime.

Just like in Vastu Shastra, there should be enough room on both sides of the bed. Also, avoid placing your bed under a beam as it can inhibit the flow of positive energy. This oversight can lead to chronic stress and mental impairments because your room's energy is pressured under the beam.

Make it a habit to open your bedroom door and any windows for at least half an hour each day. This will allow fresh energy to flow into your room. Replenishing the Chi energy in your bedroom helps bring good fortune and prosperity, aside from necessary ventilation and ambient air renewal.

In the art of Feng Shui, mirrors can be the perfect tool for bringing positive vibes and desirable energies, placed the mirror is optimal. For example, placing any mirrors in the opposite direction of the bed is a big no-no, as it's said to bring a third party in the relationship and increase marital conflicts.

Your bedroom should only satisfy its purpose and be conducive to relaxation and good health. Aside from work and ill-placed mirrors, having a television in the bedroom is also advised against. If you cannot get rid of this habit, though, then the next best thing is to cover up the TV screen when not in use or choose an installation that can conceal the TV behind a mobile wall.

Understand the Energy Map

To achieve harmony and fill your space with happiness, relaxation, and unity using the precepts of Feng Shui, you need to understand the eight essential areas connected to several aspects of your life. This is called using compass readings of Bagua to define the different areas in your space. Starting with the north, which represents career and life path and is related to blue and the water element of Feng Shui. But the south portrays the fire element and is linked to warm, vibrant colors such as red, pink, orange, and yellow. The south suggests fame and reputation; it's the light you carry inside you that helps you learn your identity and values. This direction also reflects the perception other people have of you. Since water is almost always associated with blue and black, avoid using these colors in the southern corner of your house for elemental balance.

Symbolized by the colors green and brown, which are linked to the wood element, the east relates to a house's residents' health. Using these colors in the eastern corner will improve health and balance the family vibes inside the household. In the west, best to use white shades to foster creativity and fertility energy. Other areas are represented by the five elements, which are wood, fire, earth, metal, and water. While they're linked to different colors and shapes, learning how to follow this energy map accurately will reflect positively on various aspects of your life, including physical health, mental wellness, and success in your professional life.

Use the Northern Corner of the House Strategically

Since the northern corner of the house suggests your career and life paths according to Feng Shui, you should make the most of it. The northern element is water and is represented by different shades of blue and black. Placing a body of water, such as a fountain or a fish tank, is the ideal way to garner all the positive and nourishing energies that will propel you forward, whether in your personal, social, or professional life. Placing any water body in this corner of a building is proven to induce marked improvements in health, wealth, happiness, and soaking family members with auras of positivity and harmony. An aquarium attracts fortune and financial prosperity; however, one must be careful to not botch it as this could lead to loss of income, bankruptcy, possible lawsuits, and a host of negative repercussions.

Beware of The Poison Arrows

In Feng Shui, it's believed that any sharp or pointed objects naturally channel negative energies. They can wreak havoc on your house by spoiling its balance and harmony. To prevent this from happening, avoid having any pointed objects such as sharp corners, roof angles, buildings with pointed ends, or overhead beams that might foster noxious energies, bring bad luck, impact health, cause missed opportunities, and more. Such sharp objects are often called *poison arrows* or "*the killing breath*," a fitting term for the concept.

Do Not Disturb the Flow

The energy of Feng Shui is positive, smooth, and flows. In that optic, it's essential to make sure that your house harbors no objects that might disrupt the flux of positive energies. This is why best to do away with decorative items that might be too gaudy or ostentatious and disrupt this flow. This is up to preferences. If you're a fan of paintings and artwork, adorning your space with the right pieces in the right places will help in achieving a more harmonious space. If you find that some art pieces, light fixtures, or any décor items are distracting then best to get rid of them. Don't be tempted to hang on to possessions that might push negative energies your way.

The art of Feng Shui can feel intricate, to some extent. When you're first stepping foot on this territory, it's recommended to start with the simple and easy-to-implement home arrangement and decoration tips. As you'll have noted, the aforementioned suggestions require no destruction or demolishing. You can simply start by paying attention to the five essential elements, the colors associated with them, and their overall balance to effectively transform your space into a more welcoming, harmonious environment that will foster prosperity and auspiciousness inside your household.

Conclusion

Congratulations on reaching the end of this book! The chapters gave you a comprehensive overview, so you don't feel the need to move between the chapters should you be searching for something in particular. It's always recommended to read more on the history of Vastu Shastra and Feng Shui to understand the context of these last few chapters. Even though you won't need extensive historical knowledge to design or renovate according to their principles, it will allow you to unearth the true purpose behind the different techniques mentioned throughout.

While the major focus of this book was on the principles of Vastu Shastra, Feng Shui is also relevant for many architects and people interested in learning more about the energy balance of their homes. You'll notice that you can combine many overlapping elements between the two sciences to produce something that is both convenient and original. Vastu has inspired a lot of Feng Shui's schools of thought, so drawing comparisons can show you the exact points of junction that you can take advantage of, especially about the concepts of Chi and Prana.

Most people who are interested in Vastu have turned to it because of their concern about the ecosystem. The modern world no longer has enough clean air and water for the environment to sustain itself and thrive. Vastu has become one of the go-to solutions for a growing number of modern designers and architects to reduce domestic and professional structures' carbon footprints. And while it'd be virtually impossible to force the whole world to utilize resources better, the more Vastu principles are applied, the more attracted people will become to its positive effects. The resources used today differ vastly from those that were used when these ancient sciences originated, but it shouldn't be too hard to find viable alternatives if you base your search on the principles of Vastu.

After learning about the pillars of Vastu, it's time to look inwards for ways to achieve the harmonious living you've just learned. No standard practice will miraculously make you feel in harmony, but you can always guide your steps with the balance acquired from Vastu and Feng Shui. You'll be able to associate the right elements with both your home and your workplace, and if you are an architect or an interior designer, you'll be able to effectively bring harmony and peace to the buildings and projects you'll be working on in the future.

Capturing the essence of Vastu can make you progress on a conscious level. Always use or follow those practices you understand, rather than comply with stale, outdated conventions. Relating its effects and causes will help you come closer to unlocking Vastu's true potential. Its principles can be applied virtually anywhere, whether it's a hut, factory, home, corporate offices, or even a school. It will be you who decides how to carry out them so it ensures a balanced energy dynamic.

Even though not all Sanskrit treatises have been translated to English because some were lost or produced in a dead language, there are plenty of resources that were unearthed and properly explain the major principles of Vastu. Many of the scriptures were considered at the time of writing this book to make sure that it's up-to-date with the latest translations. Also, it wouldn't be a bad idea to move on to researching specific treatises like the Manasara, Vastu Nirnaya, and many others after you've grasped the basics. If you've digested most or all the information in this book carefully, you may be ready to delve into more specific schools of thought on the ancient science of Vastu.

Since Vastu was created thousands of years ago, many interior designers and architects will find it challenging to integrate into their designs, but as you learn of the most popular methods and practices in use, you'll be able to intuitively do it because it's the natural order of things. Modern-day activities and quality of life are much more developed compared to their ancient counterparts, making it more of an interesting challenge to mix and match and strike that perfect balance using what you've learned in Vastu.

It might also be wise to integrate what you've learned about trees and green spaces whenever and wherever relevant. You should be able to understand why using Vastu Shastra to incorporate green spaces in your buildings is quite unique. There is no shortage of ideas you can implement in your home or workplace to help instill nature's vibrations in any space.

Novices may find it hard to keep up if they directly focus on implementing all the techniques and theories of Vastu Shastra. In this book, the slow-paced step-by-step guide format is enough to allow a beginner to catch up and get familiar with the concepts while still being straight to the point for users who've covered ground in this science before.

Avoid overwhelming yourself when you're trying to start Vastu Shastra in any location. It's important to understand that you must first be at peace with yourself before you can make your surroundings tranquil. Instead of recommending easier-said-than-done techniques, you won't encounter obstacles as you begin to explore the options at your disposal. From tearing down imprisoning walls to reorganizing a library, you should find the process meditative, liberating, and fulfilling.

Ultimately, as you implement the strategies detailed in this book, always remind yourself of your progress. Whether it was just a small renovation or a complete overhaul, you'll find it an enriching experience you just can't get enough of. Remember that taking well-defined and proactive steps will help you go through this life-changing experience, optimize your living spaces, and improve your physical and mental health.

Here's another book by Mari Silva that you might like

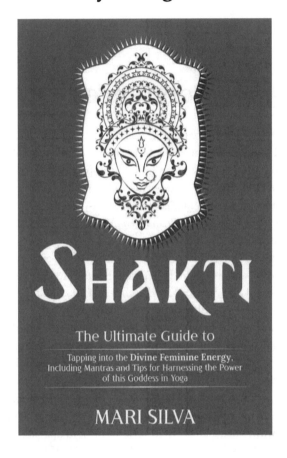

References

8 directions of vastu shastra and how they impact your life. (n.d.).
Www.Homeonline.com. https://www.homeonline.com/hol/home-tips/8-directions-of-vastu-shastra-and-how-they-impact-your-life.html

10 Best Vastu Plants for Home. (n.d.). Www.Floweraura.com. Retrieved from https://www.floweraura.com/blog/best-vastu-plants-for-home

20 Vastu tips to bring health and wealth in 2018 - Times of India. (n.d.). The Times of India. Retrieved from https://timesofindia.indiatimes.com/life-style/home-garden/20-vastu-tips-to-bring-health-and-wealth-in-2018/articleshow/62118563.cms

Benefits of Vastu Shastra | Importance of Vastu Shastra | Need for Vastu Shastra. (n.d.). Www.Prokerala.com. Retrieved from https://www.prokerala.com/vastu-shastra/benefits-of-vastu-shastra.htm

Influence of Vastu on Modern Indian Architecture. (2020, August 4). Center for Soft Power. https://www.softpowermag.com/influence-of-vastu-on-modern-indian-architecture/

Karki, T. (2020, January 26). *Vastu tips: Sitting under pyramid roof provides relief from insomnia, headache.* Www.Indiatvnews.com. https://www.indiatvnews.com/lifestyle/vastu-vastu-tips-sitting-under-pyramid-roof-provides-relief-from-insomnia-headache-583074

Livspace. (n.d.-a). *6 Simple Vastu Tips to Design Your Pooja Room.* Livspace Magazine. Retrieved from https://www.livspace.com/in/magazine/6-pooja-room-vastu-tips

Livspace. (n.d.-b). *6 Vastu-approved and Positive Colours for Your Bedroom.* Livspace Magazine. Retrieved from https://www.livspace.com/in/magazine/vastu-bedroom-color-as-per-vastu

Misconceptions about Vastu. (n.d.). Transcendence Design. Retrieved from https://transcendencedesign.com/blogs/vastu-blog/misconceptions-about-vastu

SCIENTIFIC VASTU PRINCIPLE | AAYADI (DIMENSION) | ARCHITECTURE IDEAS. (n.d.). Retrieved from https://architectureideas.info/2010/01/vastu-shastra-principle-aayadi-dimensions/

Vaastu Basics, Vastu Principles, Vaastu Shaastra, Vaastu India. (n.d.). Www.Vaastu-Shastra.com. Retrieved from https://www.vaastu-shastra.com/introduction-of-vastu-shastra.html

Vaastu Reference In Ancient Scriptures. (n.d.). Pandit.com. Retrieved from https://www.pandit.com/vaastu-reference-in-ancient-scriptures/

Vastu for office interiors: 10+ tips for success and prosperity at work. (2018, July 2). Architectural Digest India. https://www.architecturaldigest.in/content/vastu-shastra-office-success-financial-prosperity/

Vastu Purusha & Vastu Purusha Mandala [EXPLAINED]. (2014, March 6). Vastu Shastra Guru. https://www.vastushastraguru.com/vastu-purusha-mandala/

Vastu Purusha: The Fascinating Story. (n.d.). Www.Speakingtree.In. Retrieved from https://www.speakingtree.in/allslides/vastu-purusha-the-fascinating-story/brahma-asked-help-of-ashta-dikpalakas

VASTU SHASTRA. (n.d.). Www.Hinduscriptures.In. Retrieved from https://www.hinduscriptures.in/vedic-knowledge/vastu-shastra/vastu-shastra

Vastu Shastra: 10+ tips to attract good fortune with a garden at home. (2018, August 6). Architectural Digest India. https://www.architecturaldigest.in/content/vastu-shastra-garden-plants-good-fortune/

Vastu Tips: How To Attract Wealth To Your Home. (n.d.). Www.Makaan.com. Retrieved from https://www.makaan.com/iq/happy-home-family/vastu-tips-to-attract-wealth-to-your-home

What Is Feng Shui. (n.d.). The Feng Shui Society. https://www.fengshuisociety.org.uk/what-is-feng-shui/

What is Feng Shui? | An Interior Decorating Guide. (2017, September 11). Invaluable. https://www.invaluable.com/blog/what-is-feng-shui/

What is Vastu Pyramid and The Secret Behind It? (n.d.). Www.Magicbricks.com. Retrieved from https://www.magicbricks.com/blog/lifestyle/vastu/what-is-vastu-pyramid/115360.html

What is vital energy, or chi or prana? | Spiritual Therapies. (n.d.). Sharecare. Retrieved from https://www.sharecare.com/health/spiritual-therapies/what-vital-energy-chi-prana

What's the difference between prana and chi? (n.d.). Yogapedia.com. Retrieved from https://www.yogapedia.com/whats-the-difference-between-prana-and-chi/7/10313

Made in United States
Troutdale, OR
11/12/2023